100 OUTSTANDING
SUMMER CAMP PROGRAM IDEAS

THE COLLECTION

This collection of summer camp program ideas came from the submissions of three of our email round tables; "Best Programs", "Best Things We Do At Camp" and "It's a Hit!" These 100 program ideas were chosen because they are unique, creative and most can be done at either a day camp or resident (sleep-away) camp. These activities, programs and events were submitted by directors and program directors from all over the world.

EMAIL ROUND TABLES

Want to be part of future email round tables? Each month a new one is offered. Those on my email list get notified and have a few days to submit their ideas on the given topic. In return they are sent the complete compilation of everyone's ideas. This series of books are edited versions of those round tables. If you would like to participate in future email roundtable go to the home page of SummerCampPro.com and sign-up to receive email notifications.

Curt "Moose" Jackson
SummerCampPro.com

TABLE OF CONTENTS

1. DO-IT-YOURSELF WATER PARK 1
2. KNOW YOUR CAMPER TRUTH CEREMONY 3
3. THE WHEEL OF MISFORTUNE 4
4. THE GUINNESS GAMES. 5
5. KEY TO THE TREASURE 5
6. MARK TWAIN DAYS 6
7. TALENT/NO TALENT SHOW 7
8. ROCK THROWING AREA 8
9. BEAD TRADE-IN 8
10. OUR CAMP'S GOT TALENT 9
11. WESTERN NIGHT 10
12. PAY IT FORWARD 10
13. THE SPIRIT OF CAMP - CAMPFIRE 11
14. HARRY POTTER WEEK 12
15. MINUTE TO WIN IT STATIONS 12
16. CHANGE THE WORLD 12
17. SUPER SECRET GUEST 13
18. SUPER COOL VEHICLE DAY. 14
19. YOUTH FITNESS 15
20. WILD WEST AUCTION 16
21. BUTTON TRADING 17
22. ICE WATER DAY STATIONS. 18
23. MYSTERY TRIP 19
24. THEMED TRAILS 20
25. MOVIE QUOTE SCAVENGER HUNT 21
26. TRICK AND TREAT NIGHT 21
27. CREATING CAMP MAGIC. 22
28. THROUGH THE AGES 23
29. MISSION PROJECTS 24
30. KINGDOM KATASTROPHE. 25
31. CAKE WARS 26
32. BUZZWORD 27
33. FIRST TIME COLOR WAR. 28
34. CHAOS 29
35. REVERSE SCAVENGER HUNT 30
36. HIT LIST 32
37. CARDBOARD BOAT REGATTA 33
38. CARNIVAL ANSWERING MACHINE 34
39. ALICE IN WONDERLAND / UN-BIRTHDAY PARTY. 35
40. PANDEMIC - CAMP WIDE GAME 36
41. S'MORE BAKE-OFF 37
42. SKILLS NIGHT 39
43. HARRY POTTER BREAKFAST 40
44. ROTATION CELEBRATION 41

45. COLOR OLYMPIC THEME WEEK 41
46. AMAZING RACE AT CAMP 42
47. ADVENTURE CHALLENGE 42
48. MIDNIGHT MADNESS 42
49. HOUSE POINTS 43
50. RED CARPET EVENT 44
51. SAFARI HUNT 45
52. THEMED MEALS 46
53. THE AVENGERS EVENING ACTIVITY 47
54. HOLIDAZE CELEBRATIONS 48
55. MAGGOT ART 49
56. WALKING TACOS 49
57. BEAD REWARD PROGRAM 50
58. THE HUNGRY GAMES 50
59. WISHBOAT CEREMONY 51
60. I'M A CELEBRITY...GET ME OUT OF HERE 51
61. KINDNESS TICKETS 52
62. SCOOTER TOWN USA 53
63. AROUND THE WORLD DAY 53
64. PHOTOGRAPHY CAMP 54
65. DANCING WITH THE ALL-STARS 54
66. PANIC 55
67. BATTLE OF THE SUPER STARS 56
68. SILENT MEAL 56
69. WHERE'S WALDO? 57
70. GETTING TO KNOW YOUR COUNSELOR 57
71. FICTIONAL COUNTRIES - OLYMPICS 58
72. SUNNY S'MORES 58
73. A BETTER CAMPOUT 59
74. CHOOSE YOUR OWN ADVENTURE TUESDAY 60
75. MISSION IMPOSSIBLE 61
76. STAFF PROJECTS 62
77. REDNECK DINNER 62
78. HOMEMADE ICE CREAM IN A BAG 63
79. BLACK LIGHT PARTY 64
80. MAKING FAKE SNOT 65
81. THE BIG APPLE DAY 66
82. CHRISTMAS CARDS 66
83. COW TONGUE COMPETITIONS 67
84. INTRODUCING CAMP NAMES 68
85. GIANT GAME OF LIFE 69
86. STAFF RECOGNITION 70
87. THE CIVILIZED DINNER 70
88. CHRISTMAS IN JULY 71
89. MODERN ART NIGHT 72
90. BEACH THEME 73
91. WE'RE ALL GOING M.A.D. 74

92. OLD TIME OLYMPICS. 75
93. TEACHABLE MOMENT 75
94. SURVIVOR THEME 76
95. EMBERS: WISH-SURPRISE-WONDER. 78
96. ZOMBIE RAID - CAMP WIDE GAME 80
97. GAMES FOR A SUPERHEROES THEME 82
98. IDEAS FOR A WILD WEST THEME 85
99. KIDS SWAP MEET 90
100. THE PROPOSAL 91

DO-IT-YOURSELF WATER PARK

It's all the rage to build a water park at your camp these days. But if you do the research (like borrow a kid and go to a municipal water park), you'll find that kids get bored VERY quickly because even those things that are supposed to be "interactive" are very limited in creative play. So a lot of running, no making of new friends. And if you've priced one, you'll find that they are NOT as much cheaper than a pool as you would think.

When YOU were a kid and it got really hot outside, you went to the garage and grabbed every piece of hose and every kind of sprinkler you could find and set them up in the yard. What a blast!

That's the best thing you can do for CAMP, too.

Give a couple creative and "cheap" counselors $200 to go to Walmart and buy a bunch of inexpensive hoses, manifolds (those things that let 4 hoses hook to one faucet), and a bunch of different sprinklers: wave, rotary, perforated hose, ffft-ffft-ffft-rotating, ring. Whatever. A few plastic "grips" so they can be clamped to an old stepladder, a chair, etc. And then pick a spot that needs watering.

What you spend on water will be less than what you'd spend on electricity and chlorine. You move the location so different grass gets watered every day.

With the first group of campers you say, "Rats! Look at all this stuff! (pointing at box of hoses and sprinklers). This was all suppose to be put together so that you could cool off. Oh well, I guess we'll just have to come back tomorrow."

Of course at least one kid will say, "WE could do it!"

Rubbing your chin, you say, "I don't know, do you think you're smart enough to figure out how to use every one of these things at the SAME TIME?"

And away you go! Let them know you'll turn the water "on" and "off" every 10 minutes so that they WANT to re-arrange it when it's "off" to create something new. AMAZING fun and creativity and teamwork! They put it away at the end of the day and start fresh tomorrow!

WANT EVEN MORE DIY WATER PARK FUN?!

Get some ½" PVC pipe (the white stuff that glues/screws together) and have them create their own water-park spray features.

With a cordless drill and a 3/32" bit they can drill patterns of holes in a 10' section of pipe to create a wave, a dragon, an obstacle course... you can even set it along the gutter in your pool to create more fun in the shallow end! (In the "irrigation" section of your Home Depot / Lowes / Menards you'll find the connector for a "3/4 hose fitting to the ¾" pipe thread" for the ½" PVC (interior dimension) pipe.

Some of the camps I've worked with have let the kids use short hack-saws and vices to cut their own pipe and use gloves to glue them. Others cut a variety of lengths ahead of time and glued pipe-thread fittings on each end so they can be assembled and disassembled by the kids (a little more expensive, but YEARS of fun for not much money). (If you're even smarter, ask for some dads to volunteer to make the parts. Every guy is looking for a reason to go to Home Depot and spend $20 on something their kid will love!)

"We don't have grass." Then get a piece of indoor-outdoor carpet (el-cheapo grass color is fine) and do it on asphalt.

Be sure to take some photos of kids working together connecting everything! Next year you won't want a spray park any more, you'll want EVEN MORE hose!

SummerCampPro.com

KNOW YOUR CAMPER TRUTH CEREMONY

One thing that I have done with my day camp is having a "know your camper truth ceremony."

1. Spend the first half-hour making one or two friendship bracelets.
2. Next we'd gather around our group space (classroom, flag pole, etc) and introduce the activity.
3. We'd then go around and play the game Two Truths & a Lie. The game is exactly how it sounds. Each person would say to truths and one lie and they'd have to guess the lie.
4. After that we would have hobos or other snacks to keep our spirits up.
5. Then we would do a variety of small group team building activities.
6. Next we would do a trivia sort of game where each camper would come up with facts about the others and we would guess who they're talking about. The counselors are also involved in the game!
7. Finally we would hand out our friendship bracelets to one or two different people. The only catch was that everyone had to end up with at least one bracelet.

The goal of the activity is two-fold: first to get to know the campers and staff and to make everyone "feel good" because they'll end up with at least one new friend.

We tried it one time last year and it seemed to work fairly well. We did it during the last week of camp. Perhaps this summer we'll do it two or three times throughout the summer.

THE WHEEL OF MISFORTUNE

For every three letters a camper gets, they have to sing, but for a package, they get to spin the Wheel of Misfortune. If they get two packages in one day, they still only spin it once.

Spaces on the wheel are things like:
- no chair (at the dining hall for entire cabin at next meal)
- no silverware (same as previous)
- kiss Bucky (camp deer head on dining hall wall)
- dunk tank (three shots in counselor in tank)
- firing squad (water balloons at camper that spun)
- chicken space (act like a chicken for 30 seconds)
- free candy
- polar bear swim (whole cabin gets early swim time)
- kitchen raid (prearranged chance for cabin to eat some leftovers)
- pie in the face
- ring the chapel bell
- ride in director's golf cart

Mail Call has become an event and yes it takes a long time this way, BUT the campers look forward to spinning the wheel every year and don't seem to mind waiting in the sometimes 75 person long line. We get them through as fast as possible.

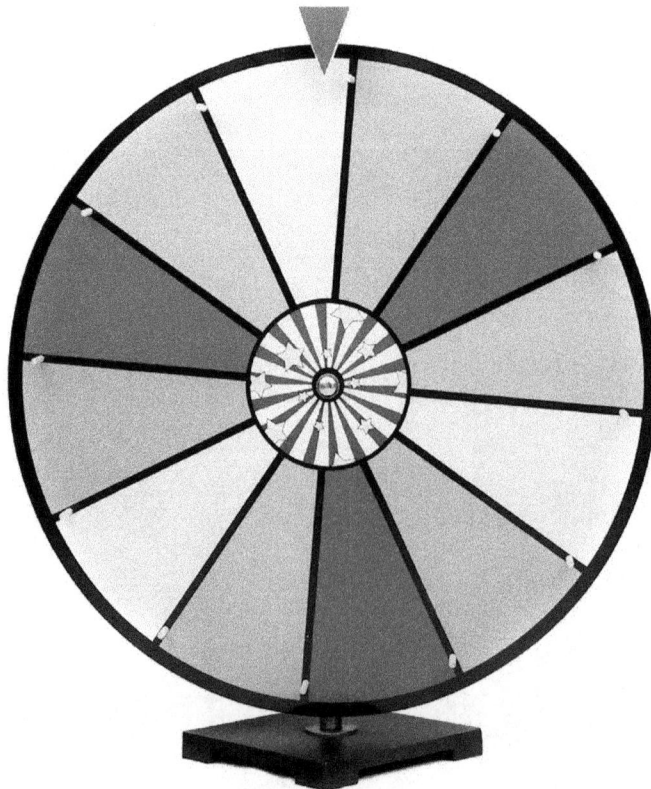

THE GUINNESS GAMES

We have been doing this since 2000 For junior high campers only.

Campers are able to set and break any record they want as long as it's witnessed by a staff member. We have a form that they fill out and turn in at the office. We then record and post the records so others can have the opportunity to break them.

Over the years we have had to "ban" food records because they got to be wasteful and just disgusting. Some records we have include (there are hundreds of records now!!!):
- longest time not talking at camp
- longest time wearing a life jacket
- longest time tapping nose
- longest time banging head on a #3 Frisbee golf sign
- most free throws
- most t-shirts worn at one time
- longest time underwater
- most shoes brought to camp
- tallest junior high camper
- fastest time from dining hall to chapel running

This works great with junior high because they are able to do the records themselves without help. The younger campers would need too much supervision and the high school campers are just way too cool to do something like this. This is a GREAT USE for junior high dorky energy. They LOVE IT! We have been doing it so long that now some of our counselors still hold records from when they were junior highers and their campers are trying to break them! So fun!!!

KEY TO THE TREASURE

We have an award system at camp to keep the cabins excited and participating in all activities.

Keys are awarded to cabins for different activities, challenges and events. For example:
- first cabin to an activity gets a key
- cabin who wins a game gets a key
- cabin that does something helpful gets a key

We have a large chest with a chain and a lock on it. At the end of the week we play the mission impossible theme music and let the cabins come up and try their keys in the locks. The cabin that is able to open the lock, wins a chest full of goodies!

MARK TWAIN DAYS

When we held this theme we had 8 units of approx. 36-40 girls each.

FIND THE PIE
During the week the girls were responsible for finding a pie (made from paper mache and painted) like the ones Aunt Polly placed on the window ledge to cool, in one of the units that had to be hidden in plain sight. The trick is to do it when no one is looking, then write your unit name on the underneath side each time you had it.

This was a fun, ongoing activity for the week of day camp but on the one overnight, we had the competitions, i.e.

FENCE WHITE-WASHING
We had some materials donated from Home Depot to make 8 short picket fence panels about 2' wide and 4' tall. We staked these into the ground for stability. During the event the girls had to use fly swatters for paint brushes and race to brush a mixture of white paint and water about 1:3 onto the panels to see how much of the panel they could cover in a minutes time. They also wore the disposable rain ponchos that you can get 2/$1 at Dollar Tree.

FROG JUMP RACE
We had 8 frogs indigenous to the area so they could be released into the creek area after camp. The frogs were lined up and the girls had to prompt the frogs, without touching them, to reach a finish line. Just know, frogs don't really cooperate well but it was a great laugh.

MINI-RAFT BUILDING
Each unit was given materials at the beginning of the week to build a raft by lashing. The materials were six 1/2" dowel rods approx. 6 inches long and twine or jute was used for rope. During the competition we had a molded pool of water to see which ones floated and which didn't.

Of course they all floated but it was a great way to hone their skills and fun to see how each unit decorated their raft. Some were pretty elaborate.

PIE EATING CONTEST
The "Pie Eating Contest" was fun which involved the unit leaders (adults). The pies were thawed crusts in tin pans filled with pudding and topped with whipped cream. We all know how a pie eating contest works. Hands behind the back and go to it. The girls loved seeing their leaders a mess and they were really good about cheering them on. Good sense of

being a team.

3-LEGGED RACE
We found a Feed and Seed store that was willing to donate burlap feed sacks which we washed before hand.

AWARDS
Ribbons were given on the last day of camp for the competitions and everyone walked away with at least one ribbon even if it was just a participation ribbon.

SPECIAL GUEST
We had a college student from a school of thespians come in costume as Mark Twain and tell the story of his life on the river with Huck Finn and Joe. This was their bedtime story after competitions to settle them and they might've learned something along the way.

TALENT/NO TALENT SHOW

Talent Shows are pretty common, but since some people don't have GOOD talents they can share like singing/dancing, we let people share their untalents as well.

We have a panel of judges who sit at the light table. (We drilled 4 holes in a table and, wired up light bulbs to light switches on the tables). So when judges like a performance or are impressed by a performance, they light up their bulb.

At the end of the talent night, the judges converse and come up with Best Talent, Best No Talent, Honorable Mentions. The no-talent performance usually add comedic relief. We've had cabins go up and eat a chocolate bar as their no-talent, do infomercials selling tap water, and horrible singing performances.

We make it mandatory for all cabins to participate so we have enough acts to fill up the hour, and some kids add in extra performances. There are also those who actually do have impressive talents, as well.

ROCK THROWING AREA

One of favorite programs in our camp is our Rock Throwing Area.

We paint rocks about 1 inch in diameter different colors. Each rock is worth a certain number of points based on it's color. We then set up different targets for the boys to hit, or hoops to throw rocks through, or different object to throw the rocks into such as toy dump trucks or buckets. For every target hit the boys earn the point based on the color rock they thew. The boy with the most points receives a prize.

This area is set up the same as an archery or shooting range with a firing line and taped off area all the way around. Sometimes the boys just want to see what will make the loudest noise.

This has been very successful for us as our camp is all boys(cub scouts) ages 7-10. We all know boys love to throw rocks! It keeps them from picking up rocks in other areas knowing they will have the opportunity to do it safely. The boys also receive points for the number of rocks they return to the bucket after throwing (they don't even realize they are just cleaning up after themselves).

BEAD TRADE-IN

I just implemented the bead reward system. The kids have responded terrifically. We are a church related daycare camp, so we added in "fruits of the spirit" for kids that show kindness, self control, joy, etc.

They earn common beads for showing up and everyday behavior, silver and "gold" beads for being good friends, rare beads and ultra rare beads for exceptional behavior.

They can trade in 10 common beads for a rare bead. I am the director and the kids can't wait to show me how many they earned in the morning or afternoon.

OUR CAMP'S GOT TALENT

This is the event of the summer for the kids. We start putting this in the newsletter at least two weeks before.

JUDGES STAND
Appoint three counselors to be the judges. Let them sit by a long square table and face the stage (**Give them a big cup that says "Coke")

RED CARPET
A few years ago we made a red carpet, it took us a few hours but now we have it for every year. Roll out a long sheet of butcher paper, and use a paint roller (like what you would use for a wall) to paint it red. Leave it over night. The next morning set up the chairs in isles and put the red carpet in between.

OTHER DETAILS
- Assign a Photographer
- Name Tags for all kids singing
- Prizes for winners
- Assign an MC and a DJ – when the children fill out the form they should specify if they are going to need music if yes. Be sure to have them all in order ready to go so you have a smooth event.

As each child comes up put on some music and flash the lights!! The MC will introduce them and say what they're doing.

We did not let the judges give their opinions at the end of each child's performance as there are a lot of children to go through and it would take too long. (This is a nice idea though if you do not have a lot of children participating).

At the end each child should get an award. We use a plastic medal that looks really cute and you could pick it up from the dollar store. The winner and runner up should get a prize!

WESTERN NIGHT

The campers rotate throughout the evening so no two groups are at the same station...

STATION ONE: ROUND-UP
We had a gentleman teach the campers how to lasso....they then took turns trying to lasso the horn on a saddle...ribbons were given at the end of the evening for those who were successful with the least attempts.

STATION TWO: RODEO
This was an obstacle course relay....barrels were set up....large tunnels (opened ended barrels) were put in different places, bales of hay to climb over..., etc...the team with the fastest time received ribbons at the end of the evening.

STATION THREE: HORSES
We had local horse ranchers bring in their riding horses and we set up an area where the campers could ride the horses in a circle path...counselors lead the horses.

STATION FOUR: CAMPFIRE
We incorporated the evening snack in our western line-up....the campers made and ate s'mores at this station.

FINALE
A professional line-dance caller taught the campers a few line-dances to some great country music.

PAY IT FORWARD

The concept of paying it forward....each child takes upon himself to do three good deeds to others within camp. I do for someone else and someone else "pays it forward". This can be done within an individual bunk/ an entire division/ whole camp.

Children learn that by giving, they receive and are a huge part of others lives. One kind word, helping a friend, cheering on another, it's endless and ongoing and can impact their entire lifetime. Children can create cards to pass on and it cycles throughout the camp.

This program is great!! It is creative as well and the opportunities for the children is fantastic!! There is the movie Pay it Forward- however I would recommend it only for the counselors to see so they grasp the idea and pay it forward as well.

THE SPIRIT OF CAMP - CAMPFIRE

Our best program is most definitely closing camp fire on the last night of camp.

This is not your typical camp fire. This is much more of a closing camp reflective ceremony. It begins with a tiki torch lit path towards the camp fire. This walk is done by cabin and campers and staff walk in silently. One the way to their seats each staff member receives a candle.

All campers and staff are in their seats at the camp fire except for 4 staff members who are positioned with an unlit tiki torch around the campfire, as if they are representing a compass. Each of the 4 compass points represent the following (as we are a Y camp): Spirit, Mind, Body, Community.

The person representing Spirit begins with an illustration (story, song, poem) that represents camp spirit. After they have completed their 3 minute illustration they pass the flame by lighting the person representing "mind" torch. This process continues through all 4.

After all 4 have shared, the camp director then instructs the 4 compass points to share their flame by lighting the candle of another staff member and the flame is passed until all candles are lit. A deep reflective talk is given about this process representing camp spirit and our need to pass it.

We also have campers look into the flame and reflect on the following: Who made it possible for you to come to camp? reflect on the new things you tried that you were scared to do? Reflect on all the new friends that you made.

After this, half of the staff members are instructed to blow out their candles. The speakers says, "think of how much different your week at camp would be if these staff members had not been here." Then the candles are re-lit and the brightness returns to the darkness.

A period of reflective songs are song and campers quietly dismissed.

HARRY POTTER WEEK

Our best program is the Harry Potter week. First, we sort the kids into their houses. Then some of the kids begin to create the house flags (which are huge). The art room is full at this time. We also have an odd sock contest. Then we play Quidditch and the counselors get into full roles and garb. The feast is made of the house colors on the tables, balloons and flags. The counselors sit at the head tables and some younger counselor serve the kids.

Food served is cream soda and butter, mud pie with gummy worms, mini dogs, jello with eyes balls, and whatever the staff comes up with. The kids love it!!!!

MINUTE TO WIN IT STATIONS

For a camp wide activity we did our version of Minute to Win It. We had different stations set up around camp with various activities from the television show. Groups rotate through the stations. At each station we provide an explanation of the activity they are to perform just as they do on the tv show. At each station a different member of the group tries the activity so that each kid gets at least one chance to participate.

It is a very fun activity to do that provides a lot of entertainment. You can keep score by giving a point if they can do the activity and have a prize at the end or you can just do it for fun.

CHANGE THE WORLD

Today I Am Going to Try to Change the World is something I did last year in my devotions program. In the morning we listened to Johnny Reid's song "Today I Am Going to Try to Change the World" and in my program I read "If I Could Change the World I Would" from the *Chicken Soup for the Kid's Soul* book.

The kids then were to think of how they would change the world if they could. They then wrote it on a index card or drew a picture. At the end of the program I read them allowed so that they would know what their fellow campers would do to change the world.

At the back of the lodge I had a big world with the words Today I am Going to Try to Change the World. I hung their cards up around it for them to read and think about.

It is a rewarding a meaningful program for not only the campers but for the staff and the counselors as well.

SUPER SECRET GUEST

Kinder program (we have 4 year olds in day camp)

Tell the kids we have a very special super secret guest coming to camp and we need to get ready for them. Hint at who it might be throughout the program.

WHERE WILL THE SUPER SECRET GUEST STAY?
Have kids dress up in construction gear (hard hats, fluorescent vests, work-belts, etc.). Get all of your recycled boxes, styrofoam, plastic bottles, tarps, sheets, tape, etc., and build the special guest a fort to sleep in. Next, have them decorate the fort.

WHAT WILL THE SUPER SECRET GUEST EAT?
If you have baking/ cooking facilities this would be a fun time to bake cupcakes or mini pizzas or something. If not, it's a great opportunity to make fabulous mud/ stick/ moss pies.

WHAT WILL THE SUPER SECRET GUEST DO?
Turn on music and play musical statues, make a conga line, get out puppets and make up a puppet show (some form of entertainment for the super secret guest).

IMPOSTOR!
Have the super secret guest show up...but make it an impostor??? Have the impostor run off with the cakes/ pizzas/ mudpies that were made for the super secret guest. Have the kids hunt down the impostor and the cakes. Have the real super secret guest arrive in time to eat the mudpies with the kids, and then watch their puppet show/ magic show/ dancing and move into the fort.

SUPER COOL VEHICLE DAY

We did a "Super Cool Vehicle Day" last summer and are waiting till next summer to do it again because we want to keep it special.

We contacted business and agencies with cool vehicles and asked them to come to camp for 4 hours. Some of the vehicles that came were:

- Huge 18 wheeler moving truck
- Snow Plow and Dump Truck from the County DOT
- A cement mixer (kids got huge brushes and could scrub the truck). It was filled with water and the operator would release some!
- Dumpster truck that picked up and put down our camp dumpster
- Red Cross Disaster Relief Vehicle
- A limousine van
- A double Decker tour bus
- A county Sheriff's car
- SWAT team vehicle
- Police motorcycle with side car
- K-9 Van with dog
- A sign company's cherry picker
- Fire Engine
- Ambulance
- State Police Car
- Mail Truck
- Supermarket 18 wheeler FREEZER truck (they brought rulers, crayons and insulated lunch bags to hand out)
- And the best of all, the County Police sent a helicopter that landed while the entire camp was at flag-pole in the morning.

The day was awesome- agencies and business were wonderful to work with – it was a ton of work to organize.

Total cost was less than $100 for cold water, ice pops and pizza that we gave to all the vehicle operators.

YOUTH FITNESS

It incorporates general physical education principals (stretching, exercise, movement) along with the educational classroom component (teaching about the food groups, eating healthy).

Each AM the kids receive their pedometers, before they go home in the PM they record how many steps they took for the day. At the end of the week - the campers receive a certificate for the total number of steps for the week!

We include line dancing, games for all ages and abilities, jump-roping, obstacle courses, etc.

At the end of the week we have a large ceremony celebrating the kids and their successes! Parents are invited to come and dance, eat healthy snacks and celebrate with us!

This program runs for 1 week. The alternate week to this camp runs with doing fitness activities in the AM and then we go to the pool after lunch for the afternoon. This camp is called Fit 'N' Swim.

WILD WEST AUCTION

The biggest hit I've had recently was a new addition to our already popular Wild, Wild, West Day. As always, we had the campers go dig for gold in a nearby creek. Usually we just allow them to turn their gold in for prizes, and that's that. The twist this year was that they could turn in their gold for money this year at the "money changer booth."

Once the campers had their money they were warned by "old-time 49ers" (a.k.a. counselors and CITs) to save their money and not waste it away in "Boom Town" because greater riches might await them later in the day.

The campers were then led to "Boom Town" which was located in our forest area but could really be in any grassy field, etc. There were stations with hawkers everywhere trying to get the campers to spend their money on root beer floats, cheap little prizes, a chance to shoot an arrow at a bullseye, face-painting, enter into a raffle for a big prize, buy some little candies at the "candy store", a bag of popcorn, basically anyway to try to entice them to spend their money…. just like the ones who struck it rich in the old west. Many of the campers spent it all and had a great time in "Boom Town." Others saved their money for the hint of greater riches later in the day. Either way, "Boom Town" was a wild, fun time for them all.

After Boom Town, the campers were led to our Hall where we had a stage, chairs and microphone all set up like an auction house. They were really minimal decorations. We just did one big red sign with "Auction House" on it. On Amazon I had bought a couple of great prizes (which really weren't that expensive, but better than the oriental trading prizes they were used to).

Some prizes:
- Various pool toys - alligator inflatable, orca whale inflatable (these were cheap but took up a lot of space on stage and looked very impressive to the campers)
- Make-up kit
- T-shirt tie-dye kit
- Nerf guns
- Some of the bigger, nicer looking dollar tree toys
- One blow-up pool

We also had some "experience prizes". For example:

- Push a counselor in the pool
- Popsicle party with a counselor of your choice
- Camp Director for the day
- Ride on the fire truck (next to fire station)
- Pizza for lunch, etc.

A spirited counselor was the auctioneer and each camper had a paddle. We auctioned off all of the prizes and the kids loved it! The ones who had their fun in Boom Town took it with a laugh and the ones who had saved money went into bidding wars. Overall, it was a really fun addition to our Wild, Wild, West Day.

BUTTON TRADING

We started button trading in 2013 and this was our 2nd year doing it. We have buttons (size 1.25) for EVERYTHING. Staff, buildings, activities, favorite camp foods, inside camp jokes…literally everything and more.

Campers collect them and wear them around a lanyard. Staff wear them on their staff name tag lanyard. If a camper wants to trade with a staffer, the staffer MUST trade with them the one that the camper wants.

It has been a HUGE addition to our camp culture and is actually a pretty decent moneymaker as well in our camp store. We sell the buttons for $1. We have a Monday Starter Pack Special where they get 6 buttons and a lanyard for $6. Then after that, every button is $1. The buttons are made for pennies once you have the button maker.

We purchased our machine from American Button Machines. I wondered how it would carry over for the 2nd year, but it was great because all of the sudden we had "vintage" buttons that were no longer being made that campers brought back. We even had "immunity buttons."

ICE WATER DAY STATIONS

Here are your options of games to play: The materials will be set up and you just rotate your group along with you through the stations. You can go back to a station if desired. Towards the end, after everyone has done all of the stations together, they can usually have some free play in the water and whatever is left of the balloons. Just keep an eye on them. There will be a first aid box outside as well. Make sure they go to the bathroom BEFORE water games. Try to limit the number of inside wet traffic to avoid a soaked floor and slips!

ICE FISHING
- Divide into two teams
- Camper will stick his/her feet in a tub of ice and try to pick up marbles with toes.
- The one with the most - wins.

HAILSTORM
This is a team relay. One team is the storm throwing splash bombs soaked in ice water up in the air. The other team tries to make it, one at a time, through the course with out hail damage (getting hit). This works like an obstacle course. You can set up obstacles to run through.

ICE MELT
Each person gets a piece of ice and the goal is to melt it using their body (except their mouth). They must hold it somewhere and must be the first one to melt the cube completely.

SNOW BIRDS SKEET SHOOT
Using Slingshots – Water bombs, one team is hunting and the other team is the flock of birds trying not to get hit.

ICE TOSS
Divide into two teams. See how many pieces of ice can be tossed into a group of buckets one at a time in a 30 second period. Let each team choose one person at a time to hold the team bucket for them.

EXTRA ACTIVITIES
- Sprinklers
- Enjoy the water
- Bubbles
- Have fun
- Water balloons

Can play any variety of water balloon games or relays:
- Toss and step back
- Hold between your legs and run/waddle to the cone and back
- Over-under relay
- Stand in a circle and call a name and toss it (get really creative and assign a cartoon name to each kid then call that name)
- Run down sit on a balloon in a chair to pop it Relay

MYSTERY TRIP

Our camp is a traveling summer camp-- which means we take a field trip every day. While that sounds exciting, the campers (and staff) begin to get a little bit jaded towards the end of the summer.

This summer we instituted a Mystery Trip. The trip was towards the end of the week, which enabled me to give out clues in the days leading up to the trip.

For example, the older group's Mystery Trip was going to this really cool movie theater / restaurant. Their first clue was a chicken (I had pre-ordered chicken fingers and French fries for everyone). The second clue had something to do with a couch potato. Looking back, I wish I had them play some sort of competition to EARN their clue. Definitely something to remember for next summer.

No one in the entire camp knew where the Mystery Trips were. The campers and counselors had all sorts of crazy ideas and theories-- even going as far as to predict what their next clue would be, and what it could mean.

By mid-week, everyone was very excited about the clues, their guesses and the whole mystery idea. Parents were even stopping me in the hallway to ask questions-- and were shocked when I wouldn't tell them!

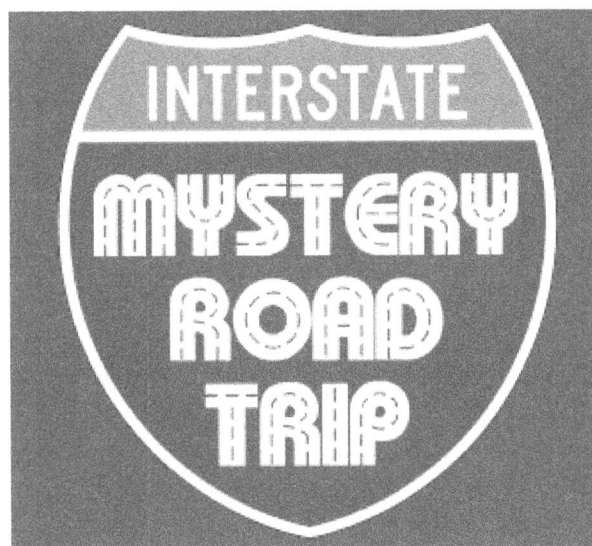

THEMED TRAILS

I have been experimenting with themed trails at camp. I find that many of our younger campers do not enjoy hiking because they dislike the mosquitoes and deer flies, or their parents have them terrified about getting Lyme disease from ticks. I decided that it was time to create a distraction.

"ANIMAL TRACKER" TRAIL

We attached animal track rubbing plates (from Nature Watch), a laminated picture, and a few facts on each animal to wooden signs. I then screwed the signs to metal fence posts, which were spaced along the trail. Then, using animal track resins purchased from Nature Watch, I made tracks in cement, painted them brown, and hid them along the path. The campers are given booklets and a crayon for taking rubbings of the tracks, and then they have to find the footprints for that animal. The campers walk eagerly to find the next post. Yet once they are there, they have to slow down to take turns for the rubbing and for finding the animals prints. This forces them to stop and take a look around them, often making other discoveries. At the end of the season, the signs and footprints are collected and stored. This idea works great for our regular campers and for our nature education program with visiting elementary schools.

Other ideas are as follows:

TREE IDENTIFICATION

Find a trail that has the most variety of trees along it. Place signs near the tree that needs to be identified. See if they can find the trees' seeds underneath the canopy. Campers can take leaf and bark rubbings. One year I had my campers, take bark rubbings in a patchwork pattern on a large sheet of paper. In the center of the paper, they wrote diamante poems about trees, and then they framed them with bark of trees we had already cut down. They had something really special to take home.

STORY TRAIL

Cut apart and laminate a book to make a story trail. They read the next page as they find it. My favorite book for young campers is *Dirt Boy* by Erik Jon Slangerup. It is about a little boy who is tired of being clean, runs off into the woods, and finds a giant. The book could change every week.

FAIRY TRAIL

I picked out a trail that has fascinating stumps, unusual tree trunks and moss for the fairy trail. Campers construct homes, dishes, furniture, and paths for fairies out of natural materials they find on the forest floor. Campers have fun walking along the trail to see what other campers have done. I hang tinkling wind chimes out of sight. There are some really neat fairy rubbing plates as well for them to collect.

AMPHIBIAN AND REPTILE TRAIL

We have some wetlands and two vernal pools on our property where campers love to catch frogs. This trail leads to this area, and they learn about the creatures they will find along the way.

FOLKLORE TRAIL

Our campers have been making loads of forts in the woods. Sometimes, it is mysterious to walk by these groupings of abandoned shelters. We build on to local tales and make up a few of our own. There's a tree where I hang percussion and chime type instruments for them to play as background effects for some of the storytelling. I may use geocaches to hide the folklore tales for this trail.

MOVIE QUOTE SCAVENGER HUNT

One big hit for us is our movie quote scavenger hunt. The kids start with a quote from a movie. They have to figure out which movie the quote is from.

The title of the film is the clue to the next location. For example, their first clue was a quote from the Lego Movie. When they figured out it was the Lego movie, they knew where the next hint would be – in the Lego bin in the rec room. Then they got a quote from ...

- Frozen (freezer)
- Harry Potter (broom)
- Up (on the ceiling)
- Finding Nemo (on Australia on a world map)
- and finally with Willy Wonka which led to our candy stash.

The kids go through it quite quickly, but you can make it as hard or as easy as you need to, and they had a blast.

TRICK <u>AND</u> TREAT NIGHT

We had a holiday theme. The thing the kids loved best was our trick-AND-treat night. We had people set up all over camp with a small gift or candy for the kids. The kids were broken up into small groups and each group was given a clue to their first destination. We made sure they all got different clues so they all went to different destinations first.

Once they reached their first destination, they were required to do a performance for the person passing out their treat. They may have been made to sing a song, such as Mary Had a Little Lamb, sing a song they learned at their campfire, say the Pledge, or recite their alphabet (something each child would know). If it's a church camp and they've been learning verses all week, you could have them recite a verse. Along with their treat, they are given their next clue.

CREATING CAMP MAGIC

One of the biggest changes that we made recently was adding the "creating magical experiences" to our mission statement for camp. Placing these three words in such a prominent place allowed us to focus on being very intentional about it.

The challenge that we gave each and every counselor, and the what we held them to by the way, was to each week have that "one" moment that they did something for their campers that was outside of the "norm." It couldn't be an activity that we already offer at camp. It had to be special, creative, and have a surprise element to it.

Each staff meeting we'd ask our counselors to report on if they had completed their "magical moment" yet. To this day, I still hear from parents, not about zip line or swimming or the great evening programs, but about that thing the counselor did with their cabin.

Here are a few magical moments that I've seen our counselors create for their campers:
- Late night camp kitchen raids
- Bringing all of their sleeping bags and pillows to the flagpole before any arrived and giving their appearance that they slept there all night
- Placing a huge blanket over their dining hall table and eating under the table as if they were in a cave
- Nighttime camp store raid
- Organizing every cabin to surround my house at 5 a.m. and singing a song
- Driving to Dairy Queen on their time off to buy ice cream for their cabin

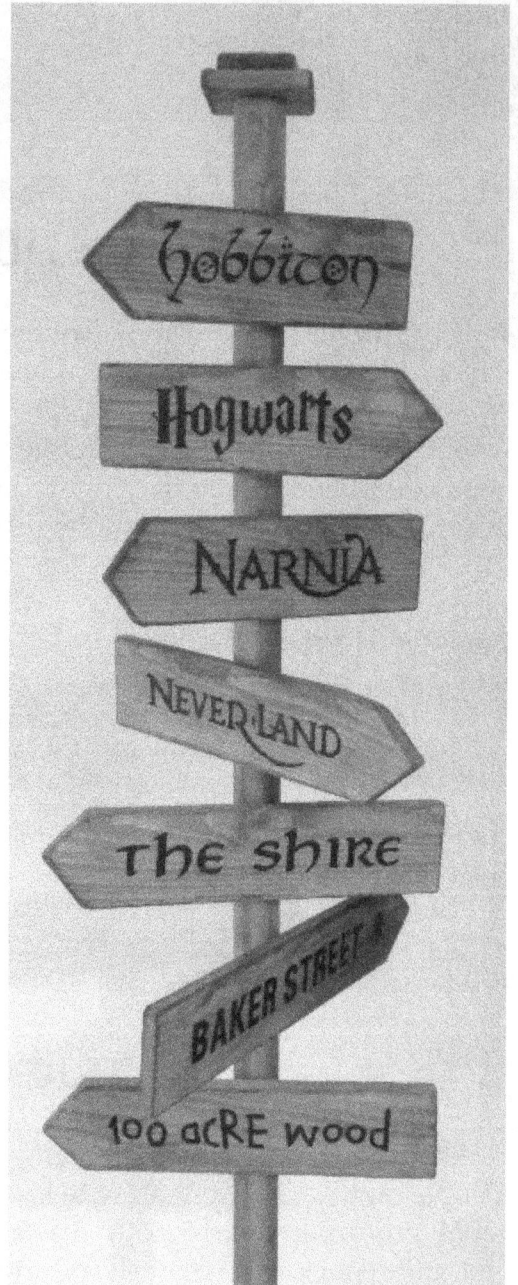

What are some of the ways your camp could do very little things that make a lasting impression?

THROUGH THE AGES

We started a new week theme: Through the Ages

MONDAY - Caveman/woman
- Campers dressed up and "Bones" were awarded for the best dressed

Activities:
- Dino tracking—before camp started we stamped prints all over camp—some leading places and others in dead ends
- A maze—best time wins

TUESDAY - Maidens and Knights
- Campers dresses up and a crown was awarded to best dressed.
- We had a fingers fest (no silverware used)—soup, campers stew and rolls—what a mess!

Activities:
- Jousting—hula hoops hanging from trees—campers run and collect hoops on their swords

WEDNESDAY - the 60's
- Tye Die galore

Activity:
- All campers tye dyed something

THURSDAY- the decade you were born (this is also field trip day—no group activity)

FRIDAY - The Future!
- Dress as if it is 2099

Activities:
- Campers made time capsules for future campers.
- We had a time machine and past staff came back for the afternoon

There was a station race that went through each time period
1. Time machine to the caveman era—here campers had to create a "home" from various materials (boxes, tubes, string—generally anything extra around camp) and former staff judged it
2. Knights and maidens here the groups jousted again—it was so much fun they asked to do it again—the twist this time—we had two electric kids cars and they rode them like a horse to get the hoops
3. Decade you were born in- we had a dress your counselor – with clothes that the campers brought in for this event
4. Create a robot camp groups had X time to create a robot from things they found around camp—one group made their counselor into a robot (think outside the box)

MISSION PROJECTS

We have one mission camp each summer. The younger campers have to stay on site with me during the mission projects, because many of the ministries we visit will not allow volunteers under 13.

The guys help my husband with construction things and the girls do something crafty with me. We have (tried) to crochet scarves for homeless ministries, we've (relatively successfully) made diaper cakes for pregnancy care centers, and several other projects.

TOBOGGANS
This year a friend with a Romanian mission asked if we could make toboggans (beanies) to send with her on a trip. It's been our most successful project yet!

Step 1: Collect fleece (search the bargain bin at the fabric store for months, hit up the clearance blankets at Dollar General, ask for donations, etc.)

Step 2: Cut fleece and sew into tubes (or get a volunteer to do it at your annual camp workday). I'm not sure the measurement on these. The volunteer was much smarter than I and free handed X, S, M, L, XL using various models (ahem, other volunteers) who were present that day.

Step 3: (Enter teens) Have the teens cut strips about ¾ in. wide and 2+in. deep into one end of the tubes. Notes: We eyeballed this. This is similar to how you make a tie together fleece blanket.

Step 4: Tie the strips together at the top of the toboggan, fold/roll the edge at the bottom of the toboggan. Viola!

We also used knitting looms to make toboggans out of yarn. A few of the teens enjoyed this, but the fleece thing was on everybody's skill level and they all enjoyed it. We even had a special needs teen that did very well with this project despite challenges in the past.

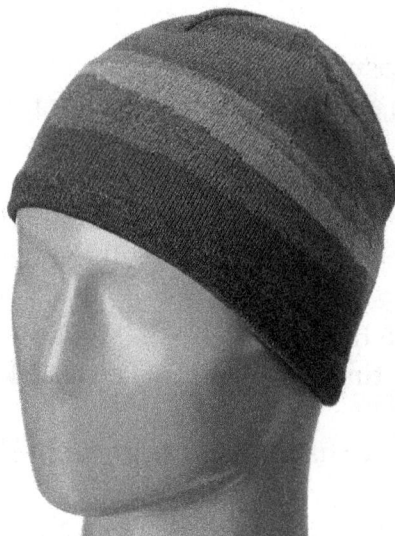

KINGDOM KATASTROPHE

KINGDOM KATASTROPHE - A Medieval-Themed Counselor Hunt

This summer (as we do every summer) we always program a theme related version of counselor hunt into the schedule. I think the kids loved this one more than any other counselor hunt we've ever done. It actually wasn't really a counselor hunt because the counselors weren't hiding, but this is what we did:

1. All our counselors had a character for the summer and our program was broken down into 2 kingdoms "battling" against each other for land domination. Each kingdom had a king, a queen, prince, princess, knights, townspeople, etc.
2. The counselor had all "lost" a part of their costume/outfit (played it into a storyline) and needed help finding it. They hid their items and then thought of their own clues as to where to find it.
3. The campers would find a character and ask them, "What did you lose?" Then the character would give the first clue, "All I remember when I had it last, I could hear running water." The first 15 minutes of the game, campers were going around getting all the first clues that they could get. The clues were not very revealing.
4. At the 15 minute mark, the siren would sound to signify the second clue could be acquired. So the process began again...the 2nd clues were a little more revealing. Many items were found after the 2nd clue. And at the 25 min. mark, the siren would sound again and the third and final clue would be revealed by the characters when it was asked of them. This clue was very revealing and all items would be found quickly after this siren.
5. When an item was found, the campers would have to return it back to the character then bring the character to the program staff to receive their points. Kings were worth 5 pts., Queens 4pts., Prince and princess 3pts., and so on.

The points were shown to all in the slide show prior to the game. (pictures below)

This is a very visually appealing game, with counselors all in costume and kids moving all over the property. It created a great atmosphere, even for bystanders. The teen campers loved this game as well. I'm not sure why this version was a hit more than other years, but the kids absolutely loved it. And it could be done with any theme, any characters created. Kids just love looking for stuff!

CAKE WARS

Campers were broken into groups of 4 with a CIT to help them. I had the lead counselors giving direction. Our elective time during the day is 10:30am-12pm for the 5 days. My original thought was to have the campers make/bake the cakes day one and decorate the cakes Tues-Thurs and be judged Friday. As it came closer I realized that would take way too long.

I called local grocery stores and tried to order sheet cakes undecorated. They all would charge me $25-$30 for a ¼ sheet cake. Too expensive!

I decided each group needed:
- 2 - 9X13 cakes
- 2 - 9" round cakes
- 1 – 9" square cake

I went to the local Dollar store and bought the pans. I bought store brand white cake mixes for about $2 each. (They are not eating these cakes so it doesn't matter how they taste.)

I made the cakes at my house the weekend before the elective started. Let them cool and didn't cover them, kind of wanted them to get stale.

I bought:
- store brand white frosting
- craft store fondant
- craft store fondant dye
- craft store fondant rollers - 1 for each group (Walmart/AC Moore)
- in the cake decorating section they have cardboard cake platters for the cake to be decorated on

DAY 1
I sat all campers down and explained we were in a cake battle to be displayed and judged Friday by all campers. Our theme for that week was Safari Week (the other week was Under the Sea).

We broke them into teams, explained how to use the fondant (Google it), how to dye fondant, and how to use the store frosting as a base before the fondant. Then I gave them a piece of paper to design their creations before starting to decorate. Then I gave them their cakes. We used plastic knives and they cut/created the base of their cakes. DON'T cover the cakes with plastic wrap. I just took paper table cover and put it over them.

DAY 2-4
The groups learned to work with the fondant, crated figures, rolled it out and decorated the cakes. Most were done by Thursday. Some needed the finishing touches on Friday (early).

DAY 5
Friday – The cakes went out to be judged. Each camper got one ticket to put in the box of the cake they liked the best. We took the count and gave certificates at the ending of the day at flag pole. I also brought in cupcakes for them to decorate and EAT!

BUZZWORD

The one thing I did last summer that was a hit (well actually, it was responsible for creating many hits) was coming up with a "buzzword" for evaluating the quality of activity planning.

Our buzzword was "EPIC":
Exciting, elaborate
Phenomenal, priceless
Incredible, innovative
Creative, climactic

We taught the EPIC concept during staff training and did some exercises in which we took existing camp activities from previous years and discussed how to make them more EPIC. We outlined how an EPIC program will engage all of the campers' senses and leave them wanting more.

Of course, not **every** activity can be totally EPIC, or it would lose its effect. It's important to choose those special moments when an EPIC experience will make the most impact on your campers. The best (but not only) times for an EPIC experience are on the FIRST and LAST day of a session (week). We called this the **EPIC SANDWICH**.

The EPIC concept really made a huge impact on our programming. We have always been really GOOD programmers, but this summer we had many more WOW moments. It amazed me how it made a difference at every level, from our counselors who plan activities for their cabin's rest time after lunch, to our programmers who plan and execute the majority of our programming, to senior staff in charge of special events.

I saw a first-year counselor who stole all her mother's extra bedsheets from home so her cabin could build one GIANT blanket fort. I also saw a senior staff member who staged a "discovery" of a pirate chest (as a set-up for the following day's colour war) that was so convincing that campers were sure it was real.

Part of what I think made this so successful was that we boiled a concept down to a single word, taught what that word meant to us, and then referred to it consistently in all of our training, weekly meetings, and evaluations. It made it extremely easy for our staff to know and understand what was expected, and this is something I am going to look at again in preparation for this summer. I'm sure that there are other parts of our training that we could simplify greatly by creating an appropriate buzzword.

FIRST TIME COLOR WAR

Here is what we tried after participating in the Color Wars Round Table. I was very interested in doing a Color War theme for one of our weeks in camp and it was awesome!

We dedicated an entire week to the event and did a number of things to make it fun for all age groups.

We kicked it off on Monday as we start the camp in our theater with the division of teams. We did this by placing color tabs under their seats that they were not aware of until we told them to take a look. We also tied our Color War to the Star Wars theme and played the theme song on the way into the theater. We had ordered special camper shirts in red, blue, yellow and green and assigned all high school counselors to teams as well. The college staff were given Black t-shirts with Jedi Counselor on the back which they loved.

On Monday the teams were given one hour together to come up with a team name, hand out shirts and create a team cheer. We met back in the theater to award our first points of the competition. The kids loved it and really got into the week. We are a day camp and were getting more and more drop-ins for the week then we have ever in the past.

Each day we started in the theater with a crazy challenge and on the first day it was the cola in a can drank through another contestants sock! Obviously we used high school counselors for this event and they got into it big time. The kids were cheering and everyone had a great time. At the end of the day Color War was all they were talking about with their parents!

As the week progressed we continued with crazy challenges and we made sure each age group had appropriate challenges that they could accomplish. Here are some examples: for the 4-5 girls we did a coloring challenge, the 4-5 boys we did a big wheels race, 6-7 girls did a friendship bracelet challenge. There were great activities the entire week.

We ended the week with a wrap-up of the Great Race. An entire age group race that I read about in the Color Wars roundtable that took over an hour to run but was awesome. We filmed a lot of it and showed the clips that afternoon to the kids at the awards ceremony.

THINGS TO IMPROVE
Film more of the events during the week, order more t-shirts for drop-ins so they immediately feel a part, definitely center on a theme, Start wars was great. Find a more clever way to designate teams. They will be looking for the tabs next year. Also, DEFINITELY keep siblings on the same team. This was mentioned last year and to be honest I shrugged it off and thought it would not matter…. It matters!

CHAOS

This summer during staff training we had all of our staff take a part of CHAOS. (This idea we learned about through an ACA conference, though I cannot remember who is owed the credit.)

CHAOS stands for...
Counselors
Have
Awesome
Outstanding
Skills.

For this activity each counselor or staff member thinks about something that they enjoy and are good at. They then think about ways in which they can adapt this skill or talent to camp life as well as how they can present it to the other staff in 15 minutes. (Example: one of my staff enjoyed beading, so she created a life-size loom and demonstrated the skill for us using large noodles and ropes, creating a very enjoyable demonstration and obstacle course. Another enjoyed learning about body language, so she showed us some great ways to relax our minds and ways to quietly and purposefully earn the attention of a group. And yet another impressed us with her talent performing Step routines, and how we could easily get our campers engaged and attentive.)

This was an incredible opportunity for my staff to gain confidence in a setting that was new to many of them. It not only gave them practice teaching but also helped them realize that they all had something different to bring to the table. This activity allowed them to see value in learning from each other and to respect each other.

I had the staff prepare for their skill demonstration and then throughout staff training we broke up the loads of information with 1-3 presentations by staff members (which was a big hit!).

Though I cannot take credit for the idea, I believe that implementing CHAOS into our staff training allowed my staff to grow in immeasurable ways, to see that they each had something to offer as well as develop a strong culture of acceptance and community. Not only that but it gave them more examples and resources of activities that they then could use with our campers.

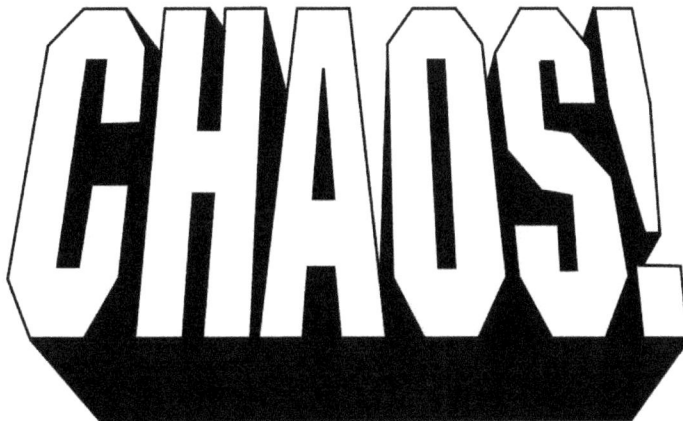

REVERSE SCAVENGER HUNT

At camp we play a game called the, "Reverse Scavenger Hunt"
Here is how we play:

1. After dinner, keep cabins at their dining table. Explain to cabins that they will have 20 minutes to head back to their cabin. They will pick one sleeping bag and put everything they think will be on the scavenger hunt list. Then bring sleeping bag back to the lodge.

2. Once each cabin is back, explain to cabins that we will review each item on the list. Each item has a different point value. The girl cabin and boy cabin that has the most points, wins a prize.

3. Only items that came into the lodge inside the sleeping bag counts.

4. We also explain that everyone in their cabin can search through the sleeping bag for the specified item, but only the counselor may present the item to their specified judge (director). If there is an item that is borderline, then the judges will confer and come to a decision.

5. Tally up the points and see who wins.

On the next page is a sample list of random items from a previous year at camp. It changes each year. Some items are subjective enough that anything may work.

Points	Item
10	Bandana
10	Camp log
10	Candy
10	Dental Floss
10	Dirty sock
10	Hat
10	Left handed hammer
10	Pajamas
10	Piece of clothing with pink on it
10	Pinecone
10	Rock
10	Shoe
10	Something that has camouflage on it
10	Glasses
10	Kilt
10	Toolbelt
10	Toothpaste
10	Water bottle
20	Leftovers from tonight's dinner
50	A piece of the creek running through camp
50	Anything with stripes on it
50	Anything with tye dye
50	Baby bottle
50	Camp song book
50	Cowboy hat
50	Missing assignments from school
50	Poncho
50	Something that you can use to start a fire with
50	Something you can use as an instrument
50	Stuffed animal
50	Tail light fluid
100	Wedding ring
100	Cabin flag
100	Eye patch
100	Pillow
100	Something that would work as a beard
100	The most embarrassing thing you have
100	The smelliest thing you have
100	Welding mask
150	Anything that has YMCA on it
150	Dirty underwear
150	12th man flag
400	100 points each: Authentic Signature of Husky, Buttercup or Scuttle
500	Cash
1000	Anything with Seattle Seahawks on it
1000	Anything with Seattle Mariners on it
1000	Picture of your family
1000	Something that is older than dirt
1000	The most awkward thing you have
1000	The most random thing you have
1000	The scariest thing you have
10000	**Total Points**

HIT LIST

We decided to try a game that is ongoing for a whole week. Other camps have many names for this game but we call it Hit List. Our campers loved it!

Mechanics:
- Each camper is given the name of one other camper as their target. You have to try and get your target out.
- Each camper is given a small styrofoam ball. Anything small and light will work though.
- To get your target out you have to hit your target anywhere on the torso with the styrofoam ball.
- Once a successful hit is made, they report it.
- The camper who was hit is out of the game, and the camper who made the hit is given a new target. Basically the target of the eliminated camper becomes the new target for the camper that made the hit.

It's important to set boundaries and times when the game is on and off. For us, the game is off in the dining hall, swimming pool area, main hall, and while activities/classes are ongoing. Basically it's on mostly during travel times when kids are walking around from place to place or free time. You play until there's one camper left who wins the game.

It took one week for the game to be completed, and we gave out a big prize for the winner. The campers loved it and wanted to restart a new game after it finished.

CARDBOARD BOAT REGATTA

We did a card board boat Regatta, and oh man was it a hit! Our teen campers made the boats, and they were divided in teams based on their color war color. Then the younger campers that were on the same color war team, got to watch, cheer and support their teen boat team. It turned out great!

Teens were given the same about of basic supplies: Cardboard boxes, duct tape and markers (we did not allow paint because they race would be held in our pool). They were told they could bring any recycled materials from home to use on the boat however, if they brought something then it HAD to go on the boat. So they had to have a plan.

We gave them one day to plan out and design their boat on paper. Then they had two days to construct the boats. They also had to create a paddle if they remembered that they needed one.

On the day of the race they all brought their boats to the lap pool. Each team had to pick a captain of their boat who would ride in the boat and paddle in the race to the other side. It was great fun and all the boats made it.

Please be sure and practice safety first - we had lifeguards on both sides of the pool and one in the water, plus each captain wore a life jacket.

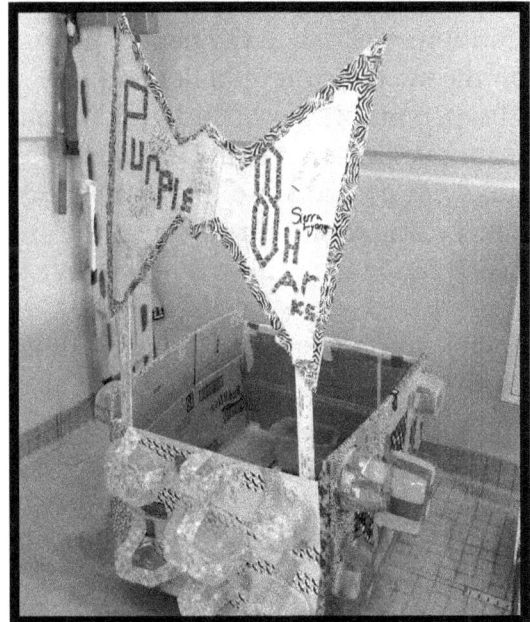

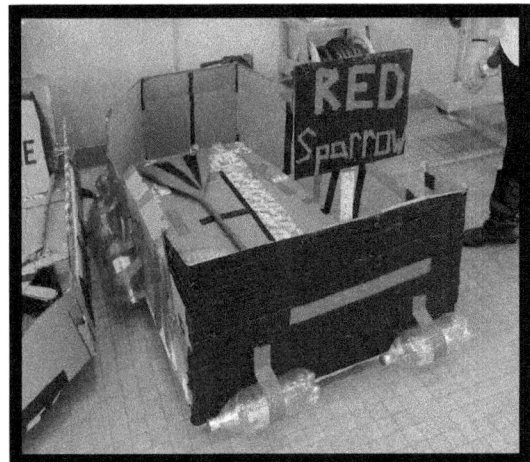

CARNIVAL ANSWERING MACHINE

We build an "Answering Machine" from a large table covered in bright paper for our weekly carnival. There is a slot cut into the paper on the front that is reinforced with another layer of paper around it. A sheet of paper is taped on the back of the slot from inside the machine. Small pieces of paper and bright felts are provided for campers to write questions on and slip into the Answering Machine. An answer is fed out the same slot.

What the campers don't know at first is that a person is inside the machine (under the table) providing the answers. Younger campers are the best with this activity as they don't try to figure out "who" is in the machine but just take great joy in receiving their answers and thinking up new questions. One volunteer needs to staff the machine on the outside, helping campers think of questions and / or writing their questions for them. The person inside benefits from hearing the conversations going on outside and can use that info to answer the questions.

The sillier the questions and answers the better. Don't try to give true answers, arbitrary and bizarre answers are often most appreciated! Answers that refer to funny things that happened at camp that week are great too. The machine takes on a personality of its own.

Caution: make sure the paper surrounding the table is secure and peek-proof, the fun depends on the suspension of belief and one glimpse of the person under the table ruins that instantly. The person on the outside must guard the paper sides from being ruined and keep campers from peeking in the slot. Provide the person under the table with some fun candy, a drink, a pillow or cushion and lots of pens. Sound effects are good, but you may need another person or a recording to provide those as the answering machine can get very busy! We place the machine nearly against a wall so that the back side of it can be entirely open to the air as it gets hot inside!

Some campers will spend nearly their whole time at the answering machine!

ALICE IN WONDERLAND / UN-BIRTHDAY PARTY

We had a few different stations for this themed afternoon. First, we gave our kids a letter from Alice asking for the kids to help her on her way through Wonderland. Our kids were sent to Alice by the water (Alice - our staff member was dressed in a blue dress and it just so happened that she had blonde hair as well, so she really looked the part), their task as a group was that they had to create the best bubble snake.

BUBBLE SNAKE (CATERPILLAR)
To create the bubble snake, in advance I cut off the bottom 1/4 of plastic water bottles, I then got a handful of elastic bands, 1 cloth per bottle and created a soap and water mixture. Once the kids reached their location they had to put all the things together to make the bubble snake.

They took the cloth and put it on the bottom of the bottle (which you have already cut out), make sure the cloth is only one layer and is secured firmly with an elastic band around it. Once it is all put together you dip the bottle cloth end in to the soap/water mixture, you then blow through the mouth piece and a bubble snake emerges from the cloth (you can add extra fun by adding a few drops of food coloring to the cloth itself to create a rainbow effect). - http://www.wikihow.com/Make-a-Bubble-Snake-Maker

THE WHITE RABBIT
Once the kids had their fun with the bubble snake, Alice told them that The White Rabbit needed their help next, so they had to go find him to get the next task. We had another staff member in a giant Easter Bunny head costume run this activity (you could use face paint and other costume ideas). Once they got to their location the Rabbit said these next few things need to be done as fast as possible because he is "late for a very important date!" Set up for the kids was a variety of obstacle courses for them to complete (you can be creative with what you do, none of our obstacles had nothing to do with the movie, it was just a way to bring the Rabbit into the theme).

THE MAD HATTER
Next, the Rabbit thanked the group of kids and said to them that The Mad Hatter (played by another staff) now needs their help at his Tea Party. At this time Alice and the Rabbit join the tea party. Ahead of time, the staff had made cupcakes and icing. The kids were given the opportunity to decorate their cupcake however they would like and of course eat it as well. The Tea Party was set up in a room that I had decorated earlier in the day. I had set up streamers, made a Happy Un-Birthday sign, and the previous night, I had other staff help me blow up a ton of balloons, which were scattered all over the floors. We had music playing so the kids could just spend some time together and enjoy their cupcakes.

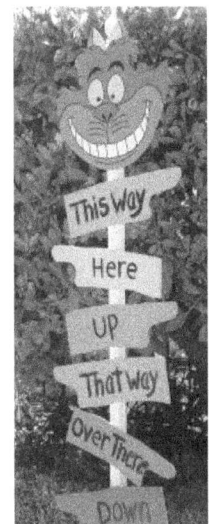

Up next we decided to play a game with the kids, we also had to figure out what to do with all the balloons; so we tied a piece of string on each balloon

and attached one balloon to an ankle of each kid and when we said go they had to go around to everyone else with a balloon and try to stomp on the balloons and pop them, the last camper with an unpopped balloon won.

LAKE OF TEARS
At the end of the game, we took the kids to the lake and explained that we were going to go for a swim in the lake of tears (Alice in Wonderland). At this point we told the kids to just go have fun in the water and swim around, but you could definitely come up with some Alice in Wonderland water activities.

S'MORE BAKE-OFF

A big hit for us this summer was our S'more recipe bake-off. We divided the camp into groups of ten supervised by 2 staff members per group. Each group brainstormed s'mores recipes and decided on one at the beginning of the week and turned in a supply list.

On the evening of the event, we assigned them each a cooking space (one of our kitchens or campfire circles) and a time limit to gather supplies, cook, present, and clean up. The groups then presented their recipe to the whole camp and the senior staff were the judges.

We had s'mores pudding pies, s'mores candy apples, s'more made to look like a campsite complete with an oreo toilet and pretzel stick/mini marshmallow plunger, s'mores pancakes, among others. The winning recipe earned an extra turn tubing on the ski boat the next day.

PANDEMIC - CAMP WIDE GAME

In creating Pandemic! my goal was to create a game that was exciting, fast-paced, and competitive without giving campers the ability to chase each other or cheat and cause more animosity than needed. Instead of groups playing against each other, campers play one team against the will of the game!

Pandemic! (based loosely off the board game) was my attempt at simplifying the idea of everyone vs. the game. In the end it turned into a glorified, and a little-complicated, themed item hunt with a reason to run around. (Rules below)

Pandemic! required some decisions to be made on the fly by some of the staff leading the game to ensure things stayed fun, fresh, and ended at the right time.

All the campers understood Pandemic! and enjoyed it a lot. The thing that made these games go as smoothly as they did was that I knew exactly what I wanted the game to look like and I gave specific instructions to counselors on what their goals were. Each game also accomplished what I hoped for in the fact that even if some campers didn't like some parts of the game, they weren't upset AT anyone about it. Since everyone was on the same team, we all win or lose together. However, we always win.

In Pandemic! Campers are now the world's leading scientists from all over and all different fields of deadly disease research. An outbreak of 4 highly contagious diseases threatens the safety of the world and it's our job here at the Center for Disease Control (CDC) to find a vaccine and cure each of the diseases. Each disease is represented by a certain color (ex. Blue disease, green disease, etc).

The way campers research and find these vaccines is by physically searching the camp for syringes. Don't worry, they are just pieces of colored paper with clipart on them. These syringes are folded or crumpled and hidden behind cracked bark in trees, in the middle of an open field mostly covered by grass and rocks, under picnic table legs, and anywhere that would be very hard to find. After all 4 syringes are found in a color, the corresponding disease has been cured! After EACH syringe has been found and brought to the CDC, enough research has been done to release a vaccine for that color! The vaccines are given to each camper with a symbol drawn in marker on the back of the hand. All they need to do is show up at the CDC and ask to be vaccinated!

What do they do with these vaccinations? Ward off the diseases of course! Three counselors, each dressed in the color of a disease are now viruses. If a camper is tagged by a virus, they must show symptoms of the disease. Symptoms are decided before-hand so everyone knows, for example, that if they are tagged by the blue virus they must now keep their ankles together. Or, for example, if they are tagged by the green virus they must keep their hands above their head. And if they are tagged by

both, they must keep their ankles together AND their hands up in the air.

They may be healed by either of a couple of medics or anti-viruses or Tylenol running around (counselors dressed in white). When they are tagged by the medic, they can be healed but often get a "side effect" of the medicine that wears off soon enough. These side effects are decided on the fly by the medic. Examples are "hug a tree and yell 'I love you nature!'" or "run and tell Counselor Bob that his guitar playing is Tee-Rific!" We also heal from the CDC. If a camper has a vaccine, however, they do not need to display any side effects from being tagged by a virus.

Every once in a while, the bell will ring and the viruses will mutate. At that point, campers need a better version of the vaccine. For the first syringe that is found in a color, campers get a vaccine that looks like a line on their hand / The Second syringe gets everyone another line, making an X. Thirdly, they get a circle around the x. And when the virus is completely cured, we will fill in the circle. Before the viruses mutate, they can be stopped with a single line /. After the virus mutate once, campers need an X to stop the virus and so on.

For the first three quarters of the game, only 3 of the 4 viruses are out running around. The campers know that the black virus will come eventually and when it does symptoms are harsh (keep both hands on feet). They also know that the black virus needs all 4 syringes before a single vaccine can be made. When everyone needs a big burst of energy late game, the black virus busts out and tags like mad! This game require us to hide VERY WELL and then give hints if syringes weren't found right away. This allowed us to control the timeline of the game.

SKILLS NIGHT

Every weeknight at our 80-camper, 4-week overnight co-ed Jewish camp we have an evening program. I decided to do a "Skills Night" program where the kids would learn a new skill. From there, I turned it over to a group of counselors to plan the details of the program and execute it. In the beginning, they were not happy to be planning this program, complaining that "it won't be fun". I insisted that people like learning new things. In the end, I was proven right. Kids loved it, and we had some great pictures for the parents.

This is what the counselors came up with:

The kids are not separated by gender, but are separated by age. 7 year-olds should learn different skills than 15 year-olds.

- The youngest group (7-10 years old) learned how to properly make a bed and how to follow a recipe to make brownies.
- Our 11-12 year olds learned how to sew (we needed more staff supervision for this one to help individuals) at various levels.
- 13-14 year olds learned how to build a fire and tie ties.
- Our 15 year olds (CITs) learned how to change a tire and would have done so if the tire iron that came with the rental van had been better. Instead, they learned that you should buy your own tools. They did learn how to find the tools according to the owners manual, where to place and how to use a jack, and how long to drive on the "donut".

The kids ended up having a lot of fun this night and this is a program I plan on repeating every summer, although varying the skills so the returning campers don't do the same thing twice. This ended up being the Evening Program that I was most proud of.

HARRY POTTER BREAKFAST

For one of our special event days at camp, we transform our community center into the Great Hall of Hogwarts and provide the campers with breakfast for lunch. We encourage the campers to dress up as their favorite character from the series and we select staff members to be certain characters such as Harry Potter or Ron Weasley, who will roam around quoting lines from the books and casting spells. The kids love the food, the decorations and the subsequent fantasy themed activities they get to do that day.

The following were some of our decorating ideas:
- Arrange the tables into four rows to each represent a House and assign the campers to different Houses via a Sorting Hat as they enter the room.
- Create each House banner to hang up
- Have a potions table where kids can taste some of the concoctions or create their own (use old jars or different shapes and create labels for them)
- Create the Whomping Willow out of brown packaging paper going up the wall (we even placed the Weasley's car in one of the branches)
- Spread out a camp themed "Daily Prophet" on the tables as well as other activity pages such as crossword puzzles for the kids to read/do during lunch
- Hang floating candles from the ceiling using fishing wire

Lastly, we projected one of the Harry Potter movies on the wall. We played the score from a CD instead of the actual sounds from the movie since we have younger campers and didn't want them to get frightened from any loud scenes.

ROTATION CELEBRATION

We are a day camp with about 40 staff members for about 235 campers. Staff are usually hired to work with a specific age group and stick with them all summer. However, this year, we decided to rotate our staff around every 2-3 weeks so they had the opportunity to work with all ages and three different Program Directors.

At first, returning staff were a little reluctant and new staff didn't know better. After the first rotation, everyone LOVED the move. They got to know all the staff better, some realized they enjoyed a different age group more than they thought, and they learned that not all camp program directors are created equal.

To celebrate each rotation, we held a "Rotation Celebration." We held a social event in town (optional of course) that counselors could attend and get to know their new rotation group or spend time with their old one. We went out to eat at a Taco place, had a pool party at a staff's house, went for frozen yogurt and did a bowling night. I have to say our staff was closer than ever and it made the summer not feel as long, since they moved around.

COLOR OLYMPIC THEME WEEK

At our day camp we have different themes each week. On the last week of camp, which coincided with the Olympics, our theme was The Color Olympics.

Each group of campers picked a color to be their team color and a name for their team. Each team was given a large banner size piece of white paper on which they designed their own banner using their team name and colored markers to represent their team color. We had a contest to see who had the best banner. The winning team received candy as their prize and was given the "Olympic Trophy" to have for the day. In the basement of our Recreation Center we found an old centerpiece that had an Olympic theme and looked like a trophy. It was made from Styrofoam and colored paper. It had the Olympic rings on it, the Olympic Flame and American Flags all over the base.

Our crafts for the week included coloring your own Frisbee and beach ball. Later in the week we used these items in some of our "Olympic" games.

On Thursday we asked the campers to dress up in their team colors using a certain sport or sport team theme if they wished. We took a picture of the whole camp dressed up in their colors and the campers we able to take the picture home with them the last day of camp. Again, we had a contest for the team that was the best dressed. We gave small prizes to the group that was voted the best.

AMAZING RACE AT CAMP

Our best and most popular theme day every year is the Amazing Race. We base the whole day on the reality show. We do this instead of colour war because I don't like the whole "war" word.

We split the campers into two teams...each bunk with the counsellors are in 2 teams. No one gets a schedule. Counsellors must participate.

They race to the "airport" for their first clue which takes them to a "country". Once at the country they have challenges they must complete including roadblocks and detours. The challenges we come up with are related to the country they are in.

They receive points throughout the day and can only get their next clue once the counsellors compete in an activity against each other, too. So the children do the challenge and then the counsellors compete in something as well. The children love seeing their counsellors get so involved.

There is so much, spirit, fun and of course messiness in this day of competition. It takes a while to coordinate all the clues so bunks don't overlap, and they have to stop at the airport for tickets after each country.

ADVENTURE CHALLENGE

We started an "adventure challenge" a couple of summers ago, and it has been going really well. It's a decathlon-type event, using a lot of our outdoor adventure facilities, such as rock climbing, archery, riflery, biking, swimming, boating, etc.

The campers sign up in pairs, and run it like a relay, choosing which of them will compete in each event. It takes about 2 hours, we run about 4 heats of 5 teams each, and we run it during youth camp. We have a big trophy that the winners get their names engraved on, and we display it throughout the summer, even in the younger weeks, to inspire campers to want to come back and participate in youth camp.

MIDNIGHT MADNESS

A couple of times throughout the summer, we wake up the campers at midnight, and have a huge bonfire, and snacks, music and dancing, and games and things. It's a lot of work, but a lot of fun.

HOUSE POINTS

One of the things we did new this year, was offer 'House Points' (we had a Harry Potter Theme). Units earned points based on participation in activities, for displaying Girl Scout values and behavior, and helping out and various things.

The unit leaders, program facilitators, and other Camp staff had authority to give points. At the end of camp, we tallied the points and awarded a Camp Trophy to the winning unit during the Parent Program.

We are going to have a banner made that we will update each year and will include the winner of the Trophy each year, so campers can look back and see when they won.

We found that campers were more engaged, more helpful, and more willing to find things to do to earn points. We did find we needed to address with some of the unit leaders that this was meant to be fun. Some unit leaders were right on top of points, others not so much, so when one unit seemed to have A LOT more points than the others, there was some discouragement. We stressed to the unit leaders, and campers, that they still had the opportunity to earn points, allowed them to evaluate the previous day when they were less on top of the points and submit points, and that ultimately, everyone is a winner, if they participated and had fun.

The biggest part of this was getting the Unit Leaders and Older Girl Caddies to remain positive about it. If they get discouraged or grumbling about it being unfair then the campers will pick that up too, and it would not work as well.

We had some negative point activities, like being late to flag ceremony, or a program activity. Things went so well, that we started flag ceremony 5 minutes EARLY on the last day. And we were cleaned up from camp and heading home within 90 minutes (instead of 3 or more hours) because so many campers offered to help out during the kaper time on the last day.

We had 'special' paper that points were awarded on...to make sure that all points were official. And the sheets needed to say, Who awarded the Points, Which Unit they were for, and What the points were for.

Our points scheme:	Points	Who can Issue
Display GS Behavior	10 pts.	Any Volunteer
Pick up litter (no tearing)	1 pt per piece	Any volunteer
Minimal waste at meals	1 pt per person	Unit Leader/Caddie
(this encourages taking only what you will eat)		
Late to Activity	-10 pts	Activity Leader
Late to flag ceremony	-50 pts	Director
Participation in Activity	up to 20 pts	Activity Leader
Special Services to camp	varies	Any volunteer
Daily Prophet submission	10 pts	Editor (camp newsletter)
Scavenger Hunt/Hike	1 pt per item found	Activity or Unit leader

I got so much good feedback from the volunteers about how this encouraged good behavior and good participation that we have decided that this will continue to be a traditional thing at camp.

We used a Whiteboard calendar turned sideways, marked the 5 columns with each Unit Color (we had 5 units) and then marked with colored whiteboard markers each day the points that were earned. This was kept near the Flag Pole so units could check on their progress each day. We asked the Unit Leaders to turn in the days points during check out, and tallied overnight.

On the last day, we had a last call just before the closing ceremony, and announced the winner. Ultimately, all units were within 100 points of each other so it was a pretty close race, and those last minute points helped to make the difference.

RED CARPET EVENT

For the end of summer we did a "Red Carpet" event. This was a Talent Showcase for our summer campers to share their talents. We had it on a Friday night and invited all the parents, it also doubled as a Fund Raiser for our new playground.

The show was Hollywood Theme and everyone dressed for the red carpet. It was a huge success! We raised $600.00 in 2 hours. :-)

A few things we did included:
- the walk of fame (children's handprints all laminated together to create a side walk look)
- having our preschoolers do art work that we matted ourselves and put on display
- sold buttons of the kids with pictures we took during the summer
- made a summer camp DVD.

The parents enjoyed it so much that I have been ask to do this at the end of every summer! Here are some pictures.

SAFARI HUNT

This is a themed counselor hunt. Take 20 staff members and have them dressed/painted as different animals. If you want to add a point element, attach a point value to each "animal" based on their characteristics (speed, camouflage, ferocity, etc.). The counselors hide around camp and the campers are sent out to find them.

THEMED MEALS

Themed meals - we did a lot of themed meals this summer, and they are always really popular. Here are some of the favorites.

STOP AND GO MEAL

The camp director and assistant camp director have a whistle, and the meal starts. Every time the whistle is blown, everyone has to stop what they are doing, and be completely still and not talk. When the whistle blows again, they are allowed to move/talk.

If anyone moves/talks/laughs in between the whistle blowing when everyone is supposed to be still, they start to loose items. First, campers will loose their forks, and then knifes, spoons, left arm, right arm (so they start to eat with their faces) and then bench, so they start to eat standing up using faces (only loose one thing at a time). The campers really enjoyed this, and the more times the whistle is blown the better.

SHIPWRECKED MEAL

The silverware is taken away from the table, and instead everyone is given just one utensil to eat the whole meal with. However, utensils are items like spatulas, large mixing spoons, ladles, large forks etc, anything but the conventional fork, knife and spoon. They have to use this utensil no matter what the food is, and they only get one utensil.

Before this meal starts, it is usually announced that the camp has been shipwrecked on an island, so we only have strange items to eat with. It is also really funny to see the kids and staff eat a chicken breast with a ladle.

T-REX MEAL

This meal was made up by a camper. Everyone has to move their arms into the side of their bodies, just under the shoulders to give themselves small T-Rex arms. I'm not to sure how to describe this, but pretend your arms are imitating a T-Rex dinosaur. Everyone has to eat the whole meal keeping their arms like this, so everyone has to bend over to cut their food, pick up their water, etc.

THE AVENGERS EVENING ACTIVITY

One of the most popular evening activities we had this year was an avengers theme.

SET UP
All the campers were brought together, and split into groups of ten and of mixed ages . One staff member was assigned to each group to supervise them.

Prior to the campers being grouped, we had a staff member dress up as each Avenger superhero (Captain America, Thor, the Hulk, Black Widow, Iron Man and Hawkeye). The superheroes all hid around the camp within a certain boundary.

Also hidden around the camp, was something each superhero needed. For example, Captain America's shields were hidden, Hawkeye's arrows, Thor's hammers (the kids were told they were able to pick them up), the Hulk's gamma bombs, Black Widow's toy guns, and Iron Man's lights to replace the ones in his suit (we used flashlights). They were hidden away from the superheros. So, for example, Thor was hiding by the arts and crafts building and his hammers were beside the dining hall.

Every other staff member was dressed up as an alien, and were hiding all over the camp activity boundary.

THE ACTIVITY
All the campers were gathered and grouped, and told by the program director that they were in the middle of a crises, that Loki and his aliens were wanting to take over the camp, and that the campers had to find the Avengers and bring them together to fight the aliens, as they were the only ones who could stop the take over.

Each group were given a map of the boundary and a pen, and had to set of to find they Avengers. When they found a hero, they explained the situation, and the hero would reply along the lines that they would love to help, but they need their _____ (whatever item it is they have hidden). The campers would then have to find the item and bring it back to the superhero, who would then agree to help, and sign the back of their map.

When the campers ran into aliens, the aliens would take the superhero's item from the campers, and tell them they could only get it back if they sing a song. answer a riddle/do a dance etc. The aliens could decided if they would give it back or not, and they would take how much time was left in the game in consideration (if there was a lot of time left, and the campers had most of the superhero's signatures they would keep the item, if they had hardly any superheroe's signatures they would give it back straight away).

The campers had an hour and a half to do this, and they had to stay with their group at all times - no group separation. When the activity ended, all the groups gathered in the center of camp, and the program director would ask who found what superhero. Meanwhile, all the superheroes gathered beside the campers, and the aliens hid around the corner.

Once all the superheroes were questioned and it turned out we had all of them, it was announced that mosey wood would be safe if there was an attack. At that moment, all the aliens ran around the corner towards the Avengers, and the Avengers chased them away. The whole camp cheered because they helped get rid of the aliens, and we knew the camp was safe!

HOLIDAZE CELEBRATIONS

The best thing we did in our summer day camp that was voted top activity was actually a theme week, "Holidaze Celebrations". Each day had a different theme and the activity pertained to that theme.

MONDAY
We divided the kids into four groups, each group was assigned a holiday to decorate for. We had Christmas decorations mixed in with Halloween and Easter mixed in with Valentine's Day.

TUESDAY
ValenEaster Day Hunt – It was girls against boys, girls were Bunnies and boys were Cupids. Staff hid paper hearts filled with valentine candy and plastic eggs filled with Easter candy. Bunnies had to find the eggs and Cupids had to find the hearts. Whoever found the most in a given amount of time, won the game. The candy was divided evenly among groups.

WEDNESDAY
Christmas in July – We had a snowball fight with crumpled up newspaper, sang Christmas carols, played "Pass the Parcel" game. (We wrapped Christmas trinkets and candy between layers of wrapping paper and on the wrapping paper was sticky note with an instruction to perform something funny, - do jumping jacks while humming Jingle Bells. The parcel was passed around the circle as music played. When the music stopped the person holding the parcel unwrapped a layer, performed the task and then got the prize.)

THURSDAY
Halloween Trick or Treating – the kids made masks in the morning and then they went Trick or Treating around to all the staff.

FRIDAY
Happy New Birthday Eve Dance Party – the kids made party hats with the year they were born on it. We had a special countdown at noon and everyone yelled the year they were born instead of Happy New Year. We then had a dance party in the afternoon.

MAGGOT ART

Yes, you heard right. Get some maggots from a fly bait place (can order them online too). Squeeze a little bit of tempera paint on a piece of paper (construction paper works well) and drop a few maggots in the paint, then watch as they squirm around and paint you a picture! Photo below.

WALKING TACOS

I get a lot of wonderful ideas off of my favorite website- Pinterest. This is one of them and the staff and campers are still talking about it- And HOW EASY!

Walking Tacos- Best meal of the summer!

Give each kid an individual bag of Doritos or nacho's- ask them to crush the chips inside

We then served buffet style the following:
- Taco meat (ground beef cooked with taco seasoning and water)
- Shredded lettuce
- Chopped tomatoes
- Shredded cheese
- Salsa
- Sour cream

We also prepared Spanish rice and had them served in plastic cups.

The kids created their own portable tacos! They loved them. Thank you Pinterest!

BEAD REWARD PROGRAM

I have to say one of the best things from camp this summer is that we started a bead reward program and it was a huge success! I remember reading about it last year in the spring and really wanting to implement it last summer but we just didn't get it to come together in time, but this year we put the finishing touches on it and it was great!!

We had several colored beads we used for different behavior rewards, as well as others that matched specific activities, and more still that were specific to the theme of each week! We too used the fuzzy beads during our "blast from the past" week, and the kids loved them!

Some of our other favorite beads were:
- Bucket charms-backyard week
- Jelly bean shaped-cooking week
- Animal charms-jungle week
- Sports beads, glow in the dark beads, uv beads and more!

To help make the idea work with our day camp program, we gave each child a chain necklace and alphabet beads the first week, then they collected beads throughout the summer to add to the collection. We had a peg board with tacks to hang their chains, and labeled them to keep track each day. We took the time during morning announcements to recognize the campers, and we rewarded them at the end of the summer with an ice cream social if they reached their behavior bead totals (which they all did!)

Watching the kids look forward to reaching the beads, keeping track of their progress, helping friends, they were really invested in it all summer and it was great!

THE HUNGRY GAMES

We had the HUNGRY GAMES, which were games based on food, of course.

- Our campers had to spell as many words as they could out of Spaghetti O's A-Z's before the other team.
- They stomped grapes to see how much juice they could fill in a pitcher.
- They had to pick up marbles in spaghetti with their feet and put them in a container without using their hands.
- They had to find food hidden in whipped cream without using their hands.
- and many more, ending with S'mores and a hayride.

The kids had a blast, as well as our staff.

WISHBOAT CEREMONY

A wishboat ceremony is where the campers make a boat out of natural material, such as a piece of bark or lightweight wood whatever will float. We then put a small birthday candle on the boat, and at the ceremony they make a wish and set their boat out to float in the lake.

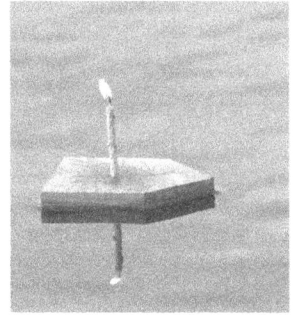

We did a ceremony specific to Girl Scouts but it can be used in any organization. We also did it where they made boats in units because there were too many campers for them to each do a boat.

I'M A CELEBRITY...GET ME OUT OF HERE

Our camp was based around the 'I'm a celebrity...get me out of here' show.

We did food tasting, touch and feel, slime boxes etc as well as cooking food for themselves using triangas.

Activities that were popular were orienteering and the assault course.

The slime boxes were simply boxes filled with
- soil and shells
- spaghetti and oil
- blamanche with plastic spiders
- an ice filled rubber glove that has had fingers chopped off

...anything really that will make the girls scream and reluctant to put their hands in the boxes. We made it more difficult by adding an incentive to make sure they all felt the need to participate - inside some of the boxes would be stars. Each star collected meant more food for the team!

As for the assault course, we led the girls to a wooded area, gave them some logs, sticks, string and tarpaulin. Each patrol had to assemble their own obstacle and then everyone took a turn at the completed assault course. Everyone had to vote which obstacle was the best.

KINDNESS TICKETS

One of the issues we had in the past was our kids not being exactly "kind", you know the usual "this is mine", "I don't wanna play with them", etc. So I came up with Kindness Tickets that the kids could earn during the summer. Granted, the idea worked very well for our 5K-2nd grader group (not for the very little ones) but you could still try and implement it with all ages.

The children earned them by being caught in the act be an adult (i.e. in the beginning the kids would do something nice and then go tell the teacher expecting a ticket…doesn't work that way)

It looked like this:

KINDNESS TICKET

_____
(name)

Helping a friend   _____

Speaking Kind   _____

Words   _____

Sharing   _____

Playing Nicely   _____

_____
(teacher signature)

**We had prizes after you earned so many. For example:

3 tickets =   Candy/Cookies

10 tickets=   Ice Cream Sandwich

20 tickets=   15 minutes Wii time

35 tickets=   Trip to Cherry Berry (which is a local yogurt shop in our town)

The kids could choose whether to cash their tickets in early or they could hold on to their tickets and earn the larger prizes (i.e. Wii and Cherry Berry). When you turn in the tickets you loose them, they are placed in the ticket muncher (i.e. the shredder).

SCOOTER TOWN

Our school has the square scooters that campers can sit & roll around on. We turned our cafeteria into " Scooter Town" with different stations (shops) that the kids could stop and visit as they roll through the town. The kids also acted as the employees at the different stations.

1. DMV – Kids could get a license to operate their scooter by passing an obstacle course
2. Hospital- We had toilet paper rolls where kids could wrap up their injuries and mats to lay on when "injured"
3. Gas Station- Orange Cone with jump ropes hanging out of the top of the cone as the gas pump
4. Restaurant- Play food , aprons & table. Post it notes to take order and a kid created menu
5. Snack Shack- We had a drive through where kids could get juice & a little snack
6. Bowling Alley – We used a plastic bowling set and masking tape to make lanes
7. Starbooks- hot cocoa, books to read & some cozy chairs
8. Mall- Dress up clothes

AROUND THE WORLD DAY

Each child received a small passport (made out of construction paper and computer paper). They wrote their name on it and decorated the cover however they wanted (with crayons, markers, stickers, etc.).

Then they took a journey to different countries. Each country was set up in a different room. Each staff member was assigned a country to lead the activity. (Some of them even dressed to match the country they were teaching!) When the children arrived at their country they got their passport stamped and they had to write the name of the country down and color in a picture of that country's flag (on the same sheet in the passport as the stamp).

Each country had a different activity relating to the country. We tried to incorporate music and food as much as possible. The four countries we "traveled" to were Japan, Mexico, Australia, and England. In Japan we learned to write our names in Japanese and ate a treat with chopsticks. In Mexico we danced the "Mexican Hat Dance" and tried a tamale. In Australia we threw "Boom-a-Rangs" and ate Lamingtons. In England we talked in our best British accents and drank tea.

There are MANY other countries we could have traveled to and next summer we will "visit" new countries!

PHOTOGRAPHY CAMP

Photography Camp - 8-12 yr olds
1 Week Day Camp 7:30am -5:30pm

This camp was lead by a local photographer with at least 2 additional counselors at all times. Campers were required to bring their own digital camera, SD card (if used), USB/Flash drive cords to connect to computer and extra batteries.

- Campers learned to enlarge/shrink photos, digitally enhance, put them in collages, and print pictures.
- Campers went on scavenger hunts around the facility and grounds.
- They went on a field trip to a local park to get some great nature photos too.
- They were also exposed to the history of photography. The instructor brought in some old cameras and books on photography that the campers could look at. They each got to take several pictures with the Polaroid camera too and watch that develop!

Backdrops/Props/Lights were always set up and encouraged to be used by the instructor.

Photos were left at camp each day and added to their "portfolio". On the final day all of the photos were bound together with GBC binding and made into a real portfolio for the campers to take home!

DANCING WITH THE ALL-STARS

At dinner Wednesday night we put the male names in one cup and the female names in another. Then we announced the first ever Dancing with the All-Stars. The names would be randomly drawn by campers that night at dinner and paired up. They would have until Friday night to come up with alter-egos and dances to "wow" the judges and the audience. The judge's scores would then select the top 3 and the audience would pick the winner from the top 3.

THE KIDS WERE PUMPED! The counselors got really into it because they had no idea we were doing this evening program! They practiced their dances really hard and we wrote up little bios on each alter-ego.

Our camp directors and a couple counselors filled in as judges while other admins "hosted" the event. We downloaded the theme music and made the trophy to look like the real mirror ball. Two of our counselors dressed up as our owners to steal the show and win the night! Our kids keep requesting this one for next year.

PANIC

This game is about as much fun as you can have with very little preparation (although cabin clean up is a must afterwards).

- The person running the activity announces what campers must wear/bring/sing, etc. for each round. For example, '2 campers wearing blue socks, green shorts, a red sweatshirt, and 3 baseball hats.' You can require just one camper per cabin to dress up each round, or involve as many as you want from each cabin.
- Campers wait in their cabins and listen to announcements of what is needed to play each round of PANIC.
- Then they panic and dress up their person or persons as quickly as possible.
- A place is designated for each cabin to run to when they have fulfilled the requirements of each round. The first cabin to get the right number of people there with the correct stuff win points for that round (1st place = 10, 2nd place = 5, etc.)

You can really get silly and creative with this- the sillier it is, the more they like it. Campers and counselors usually wear their bathing suits and put everything else on over them. We also give them time between rounds to put their clothes back.

The cabin gets pretty messy, but they love the game. You can also give bonus points for an end of game cabin inspection.

Here are some examples of different rounds.

1. 2 campers wearing all red...ready...GO!
2. 1 camper and 1 counselor dressed exactly the same...ready...GO!
3. 2 campers carrying 5 pairs of shoes...ready...GO!
4. ALL campers with towels on their heads...ready...GO!
5. 1 counselor wearing "camp name" items (hat, shirt and shorts)...ready...GO!
6. 3 campers wearing jeans, sweatshirt, hat and sneakers with no socks...ready...GO!
7. 1 counselor with a staff manual...ready...GO!
8. 1 camper dressed as "the director"...ready...GO!
9. ALL campers dressed in white togas (sheets)...ready...GO!
10. 4 swimsuits carried by one camper...ready...GO!
11. 1 counselor carrying 1 camper in a sleeping bag...ready...GO!
12. 1 camper with a life-jacket on and buckled...ready...GO!
13. 2 campers dressed in a blue t-shirt, red shorts, one flip-flop and one sneaker...ready...GO!
14. 6 campers dressed as the rainbow...ready...GO!
15. 4 campers dressed as famous athletes...ready...GO!

BATTLE OF THE SUPER STARS

Each summer we hold an athletic competition for boys and girls in grades 3-6 held on Wednesday mornings. We call it "Battle of the Super Stars".

This program is designed to have youth compete against each other as an individual through a variety of sporting challenges. The "All Sport Champion" is the participant with the most points at the completion of all challenges or events.

The Awards Presentation is the time where we recognize the youth with awards, medals, ribbons, prizes and trophies for their placing in the events. The All Sport Champion receives a T-Shirt.

First off we give each participant 5 points just for showing up. Then we use the following point scale for placing: 10-8-6-4-2-1

The events are not associated with National Competitions and intended for this program only.

Events:
- Punt, Pass and Kick
- Pitch, Hit and Run
- Obstacle Course
- Run, Jump and Throw
- Basketball Skill Challenge with a Hot Shot and Free Throw Contest
- Putt, Chip and Drive
- Backyard Games: Horseshoes, Bean Bags and Lawn Golf

End with the Awards Presentation.

SILENT MEAL

We had a silent meal during our Epic week where all the tables were rearranged into Hogwarts style seating in their 4 teams, the dining hall was decorated and huge points were on offer for the team that could stay silent the longest.

Other leaders at the camp were skeptical about whether the children would sit in silence for an entire meal and still find it enjoyable but the results were astounding.

Every team lasted 35 minutes until one of them finally spoke . . . and it was a counselor that spoke first. After one of our meal time games, they shouted "No!" when their block tower collapsed.

The winning team lasted 55 minutes into the meal before they spoke, only after all the other teams were out. This (strangely) was a highlight for a lot of the children that week as it was something we had never done before.

WHERE'S WALDO?

This is your basic 'run around and find all the items' game. We had 5 of our counsellors dress up as Waldo, Wenda, Odlaw, Woof and Wizard Whitebeard and hide all over camp.

We also made some of the items that Waldo loses (binoculars, books, camera, bone, key, etc) out of paper, laminated them and placed them around camp. We gave each of the characters a bingo dabber and tied a bingo dabber beside each of the paper items. Each group of campers, accompanied by a counsellor, was given a sheet that told them what they needed to find and a space for a mark from the bingo dabber. Once they had all of the items, they returned to the porch for snack time.

For this game, make sure that you have many different coloured bingo dabbers to avoid cheating! We made most of the costumes ourselves with old t-shirts and fabric paint (and awesome finds from the local thrift stores!). Woof's tail was a painted stuffed sock and Wizard Whitebeard's staff was a length of pvc pipe covered in coloured duct tape from the dollar store. This game was relatively inexpensive and it took a little over an hour for the campers to finish.

GETTING TO KNOW YOUR COUNSELOR

As the new staff comes together for training - prior to the start of camp - have each counselor make a poster collage that includes their photo (suggest a funny baby picture), their hobbies, nick names, their favorite foods, sports, etc. Provide stickers and colorful markers and encourage the staffers to add items from home (college logo, pet photos, food wrappers, etc).

When campers are assigned to their counselors on Mondays, the counselor can present the poster which will undoubtedly initiate conversation. Rather than going immediately to the camper inquisitions, let the kids ask questions of their leaders. This is a great ice breaker and gives the nervous campers a few minutes to hear others "talk". After the kids learn about their counselor - it's easier to get them to open up about themselves to their peers.

FICTIONAL COUNTRIES - OLYMPICS

We really had fun with our Olympic-themed week by adding a twist to it. Instead of assigning each team a country to represent during the competition, we had the teams create their own fictional country.

We added an extra day at the beginning of competition to allow time for the campers to put their thinking caps on. Each team had to decide upon a name for their country, describe its landscape, wildlife, climate, population, government, economy, etc. They also created a country flag, a national anthem, country cheers, and a country plaque. All of these items were handed in and scored as part of the competition.

The campers then performed their national anthems as well as a country skit in the final competition. The skits were scored based on specific criteria regarding how well their production educated the audience on their county, as well as on participation and entertainment factor. There were many scoring factors that allowed for many opportunities to score for one's country. Even if a specific group didn't have the most entertaining skit, they could still score lots of points if they included educational information about their country. In reverse, those who weren't very educational could still score points based on entertainment value. This helped every country to score lots of points and made the campers very happy.

I highly recommend trying this version of Olympics for a fun twist. The campers were really invested in the competition because they created these countries instead of just being assigned a country. Seeing what they came up with was fun and exciting.

I have to say, this was one of the funniest activities I've put together in a long time. The kids at our camp were broken up into three teams (as we didn't have too many campers). They chose the following country names: Doga&CatLandia, Hallowenia, and Rolling Hills. Just from looking at these names, you can imagine the creative things they came up with for their skits! It was a laugh and a half! The kids loved it as well as the staff.

SUNNY S'MORES

No campfire at our camp - but that didn't stop us from making s' mores!

I found flat marshmallows at the grocery store and the campers built their s'mores on a paper plate; layering a graham cracker, a marshmallow, and 3 Hershey squares. The sun melted the chocolate quickly - and the campers then topped their s'more off with a second graham cracker square.

This version provides ALL the regular sticky mess that campfire s' mores do. Sticky fingers, chocolate faces and lots of happy campers.

A BETTER CAMPOUT

This change/addition to our program brought a huge shift of opinion in the campers. We reevaluated the purpose of campout and made some changes to stay in line with our mission and goals. Before these changes about 50% of our campers dreaded a night in the woods. Now less than 10% have anything negative to say.

First of all, our mission and goals center around real relationships first and experiences second. Don't get me wrong, we do both very well, but the experiences, skill classes and special events, are designed to be tools in the hands of our staff as they make lasting impressions on campers.

Previously, campout was not doing that. Our staff would spend the entire evening struggling to build a fire big enough and hot enough to cook hobo dinners for groups as big as 30. Other staff members would struggle to get the big tarps strung up so they could have shelter. The greatest struggle was spending time with the campers while trying to accomplish these tasks. They simply could not find a good way to involve all the campers (and manage their behavior).

THE CHANGES
First, we decided to campout as individual cabins, instead of cabin groups. This made the groups much smaller and easier to manage, the fires could be much smaller, the amount of shelter was greatly reduced, and the campers were guaranteed to interact with their cabin counselors… they were the only staff present!

Next, we changed the menu from hobo dinners, with raw ingredients that had to be completely cooked in order to be safe to eat, to hot dogs, chips, fruit, and s'mores. Although we lost the cool element of really cooking a meal, this change also reduced the size of the fires needed, the amount of heat needed, and the cook time. It also reduced the amount of prep the kitchen had to do and the amount of time counselors and campers spent making their meals. Our beef franks are already cooked so they just need to be heated up over the fire. A few campers were disappointed that they weren't making hobos, but the majority never said a word.

Third, we made two small fire pits at riflery and archery and used the covered structures as camping shelters. These are elevated decks with shed roofs. All I needed to do was cover three sides with tarps and I had a great shelter. This provided a greater sense of safety and security.

Lastly, we had our staff come up with activities they could do after dinner. They did scavenger hunts, played Frisbee, went spider hunting (lots of fun if you know what you're doing), and so on.

With all of these changes we were able to give almost an hour and a half back to the staff to spend time with their kids. We reduced the time needed to build a fire (and the time campers had to hunt for firewood), the time needed to cook, and the amount of time necessary to build adequate shelter. We increased the fun factor by reducing the time of the aforementioned tasks, increased the sense of safety and security, and we gave the campers their counselors back. The staff were much happier with the lightened burden and they loved having so much more time to hang out with their campers. This summer campout was frequently mentioned as the favorite activity on camper evaluations were it was almost completely absent before.

Again, this isn't ground breaking, but by evaluating a struggling activity, that was almost scratched, we were able to revise and revitalize something we feel is a huge part of overnight camp and a much lacking experience for the majority of kids today.

Now campout is a highlight for a lot of our campers, much more relaxing for our staff, and it is in line with our mission. Don't be afraid to look at what you are doing and pass it through the filter of your mission. When we are preparing to make a change, we always ask ourselves these questions: How big of a tradition is this thing we are about to change, how big of a reaction will changing it make, and will anyone remember the "old" way two years from now?

CHOOSE YOUR OWN ADVENTURE TUESDAY

Our "Choose Your Own Adventure Tuesday" was a big hit this summer in our Day Camp. It was simply a way for the staff to choose to teach/program one of their own special talents/skills and for the kids to sign up to try something that they have always wanted to try, or to step out of their comfort zones. We ran two morning sessions: the first from 9:30-10:30am, and the second from 10:30-11:30am.

At opening, using a white board, counselors named the topic of their session, and as kids arrived in the morning they signed up for two of the eight sessions offered. We offered sessions like Zumba, yoga, tie-dye, drama, beadwork, weaving, archery, etc... whatever the staff wanted to share that can be done in a small group and was much more fun to teach to kids who were truly interested!

MISSION IMPOSSIBLE

Nighttime version: Mission Impossible Game:

This game is not new but we found it needed some upgrading: We built a wooded 4 post tower structure erected so that a platform capable of holding 6 Adults was built 10 feet in the air. The 4 support poles were from trees cut and skinned off our own land. The poles were cemented into 50 gallon drums and then greased so that no accidental climbing of the poles took place. (Insurance reason's). The game was played at night where 4 - 6 staff were given access to the platform (via a ladder).

All staff had high powered flashlights with momentary on/off buttons. The campers were brought to a location far away from the tower and given instruction that several buckets of specially painted rocks were gathered in milk crates marked with glow sticks at 6 locations around the camp property. Their task/objective was to find the crates marked with glow sticks and take one of the specially painted rocks and make it to the tower and place it in the suspended crate below the tower without being hit by the beam of a flashlight. The more rocks placed in the suspended crate would cause a lever to raise the prize bucket to be raised up. Once the prize bucket reached a certain level the campers won!

Anyone caught would have to give up their rock and find another bucket and start over. Staff would then return the confiscated rocks to the various buckets around camp.

Additional staff were scattered through out the camp with flashlights to keep participants active and playing the game. We found the older the kids, the better the game. Our kids seem to love the staff against camper style of game.

If the prize bucket reached a certain level the campers were able to conquer the staff and win the game. (never happened). Time frame 30 - 45 minutes. Campers wear dark clothing, staff were restricted to take only so many steps to capture a camper.

STAFF PROJECTS

One of our best ideas from last year's staff training was to give each team (a combination of program and support staff) a project that they could create, develop and hopefully complete before the end of the week. We wanted them to have some ownership over a project that benefited camp and could see what it took to get it up and running. The projects were:

- Rebuild canoe racks at the lakefront.
- Build new steps to our lakeside fire pit.
- Renovate our tuck shop (camp store)
- Fundraise for a staff entertainment fund. (They baked each evening and held a bake sale at a local grocers in town and raised over $500.)

Camp benefited from 3 completed/1 nearly completed projected and the team was quite energized by it all.

REDNECK DINNER

Our best themed meal was for our last Youth Camp (ages 14 to 16). We had a redneck theme.

The banquet meal consisted of pulled pork sandwiches, potato salad, cole slaw and corn on the cob, followed by a redneck dance on the basketball court lit by the headlights various trucks.

We also had a tailgate with Walmart generic pop, corn dogs, spam and cheese wiz on crackers, beef jerky and other wonderful appetizers.

HOMEMADE ICE CREAM IN A BAG

After combining the ingredients, each camper shakes up his or her own bag of ice cream.

Ingredients
- 2 tablespoons sugar
- 1 cup milk or half and half
- 1/2 teaspoon vanilla extract
- 1/2 cup rock salt
- Ice cubes (enough to fill each gallon-size bag about half full)
- 1 pint-size Ziplock bag
- 1 gallon-size Ziplock bag

Instructions
1. Combine the sugar, half and half, and vanilla extract in the pint-size bag and seal it tightly.
2. Place the salt and ice in the gallon-size bag, then place the sealed smaller bag inside as well. Seal the larger bag. Now shake the bags until the mixture hardens (about 5 minutes). Feel the small bag to determine when it's done.
3. Take the smaller bag out of the larger one, add mix-ins, and eat the ice cream right out of the bag.

Each camper/counselor makes their own ice cream! While shaking the bags you can pair up – toss them back and forth, sing favorite camp songs and more!! Note: Do not use "cheap" Ziploc style bags, the salt will permeate the inner bag and you'll have very salty tasting ice cream. Ice cream can be put in dish and toppings added or you can eat it right from the bag, adding topping directly into the bag – a "walking" ice cream sundae!

BLACK LIGHT PARTY

Every year during the week of camp our Sr. Campers (grades 10 – grad) host a party for our Jr campers (grades 6-9). The party is usually a themed party. Complete with costumes.

This year we had a Black Light Party.
- We filled the lodge using 2 large black light fixtures.
- The campers wore florescent clothes (many were made in crafts class during the week)
- We also had glow sticks, bracelets etc.
- The Sr's (with assistance of our kitchen staff) made glow in the dark (black light) treats.

It was a very easy party to set up and run.

MAKING FAKE SNOT

As disgusting as it might sound to some people, let's make some fake snot! Snot actually serves an important purpose in our body so this experiment is not all about grossing out our friends, although that's certainly part of the fun.

What you'll need:
- Boiling water (be careful with this)
- A cup
- Gelatin
- Corn syrup
- A teaspoon
- A fork

Instructions:
1. Fill half a cup with boiling water.
2. Add three teaspoons of gelatin to the boiling water.
3. Let it soften before stirring with a fork.
4. Add a quarter of a cup of corn syrup.
5. Stir the mixture again with your fork and look at the long strands of gunk that have formed.
6. As the mixture cools slowly add more water, small amounts at a time.

What's happening?
Mucus is made mostly of sugars and protein. Although different than the ones found in the real thing, this is exactly what you used to make your fake snot. The long, fine strings you could see inside your fake snot when you moved it around are protein strands. These protein strands make snot sticky and capable of stretching.

THE BIG APPLE DAY

We separated the grounds into 4 quadrants: Harlem, Brooklyn, Lower East Side, and the Bronx. Each quadrant had 3-4 games that the kids could choose to play, and the campers were in each quadrant for 30 minutes.

The games were:
- stickball
- jacks
- shuffleboard
- marbles
- kick the can
- punch ball
- dodge ball
- stoopball
- box ball

We also had a sprinkler set up as a fire hydrant, as well as a big piece of plywood as a graffiti wall. We created NYC subway tickets and punched holes in the tickets when the camper did the activity. We also had NYC themes music over the PA all afternoon.

CHRISTMAS CARDS

Every year after the Christmas Holiday I buy boxes of discounted Christmas cards. Then, before my counselors leave for the summer I have them sign dozens of Christmas cards for their campers. Then surprise! In the middle of winter, each camper receives a Christmas/Holiday card from their summer camp counselor.

This not only surprises the camper, it reaches the household prior to next year's summer camp planning. Cheap, personal marketing!

COW TONGUE COMPETITIONS

We did different games using 3 cow tongues. Yes, real cow tongues. You can get them at a butcher. We do boys vs girls all week. We play different games and for each win they get a point.

OVER/UNDER
We had the boys and girls line up in 2 different lines. Girls in one line boys in the other. We start by I have the cow tongues in a bucket so the kids can't see them.

We explain that the game is called over and under. The first person has to go over their head, the second between their legs, 3rd over head and so on. When we say go the 1st person then reaches into the bucket and away they go. It is funny to see the faces of the kids. Have your camera ready!!!

RELAY RACE
Relay race with the cow tongue. The tongue becomes the baton.

SQUISHY BATH
This one I picked up at Toys R Us (some Walmarts have it in the toy area). You put the powder in water and it makes slime. One box will do half a bath full of slime.

We got green and called it cow boogers. We placed the slime in a plastic container. I would recommend a heavy duty rubber made container (as one of our girls broke our container). Then we put the cow tongue in the slime.

We then had the kids again line up by dorm. We would yell out a cabin numbers by age group. Then they run to bats (dizzy bats) put their foreheads on the bat and spin 7 times. Then they run to the container and who ever finds the tongue first gets a point.

You will have to have someone recording points and someone to hold on to the container just so the kids don't knock it over. So, if I yell "One!" then the cabins that are designated as "one" run to the bats, spin, then try to get the tongue.

INTRODUCING CAMP NAMES

The best thing that we did was to introduce camp names. I worried that it wouldn't catch, but we prepared the staff for this change ahead of time and while it took a while to get used to calling old friends by a new name, the kids latched on really quickly and it became natural far faster than I thought. I got the inspiration to do camp names from the online summer camp community and I highly recommend you do the same.

Because it was the first time, some names were organic from years past, but many had a hard time coming up with names. We printed the list of 350 camp names from Curt's website to help them. On the third day of Staff Training, each counselor gave the senior staff a list of three names they would like, in order of preference, and we chose for them. Salsa, Penguin, and Mouse Trap are among my favorites. Mine is Old Man, because at the age of 29, I'm old to most of the people at camp.

One big push for the staff to love and use the names was that (without telling them), before we gave them their staff shirts, we took them into town and had their camp names printed on the back like on a sports jersey. They were so excited they immediately put them on that night and there was an impromptu dance party. Only at camp, right?

Later during camp, many campers tried to write their own camp names on their camp shirts, like their counselors. Many of our staff added their camp names to their Facebook names. It's even made it hard to tell camp stories to people who weren't at camp this year because we forget to use their real names.

We "officially" gave them their camp names at the beach before sunrise one morning around a fire. We then went on a silent canoe trip to watch the sun rise. While waiting, I talked about the importance of doing programs that the campers will remember. The CIT counselors gave their CITs camp names on the last day of camp.

GIANT GAME OF LIFE

I printed "squares" to land on coloured pieces of paper, and then taped them to the floor. Each camper had made a paper "piece" to move along the board so it didn't get crowded.

My camp is for teens with disabilities, so it was catered to that population. The game started with high school squares, such as "be in the school play and earn $5 from grandparents", "Rip shorts at summer camp and have to pay $15", and "take a great photo and have it published in the newspaper.. Yahoo!".

You then chose if you were going the Job Training route or the Community route. Job Training included things about resume writing, interviews, interview clothes, and a few community things like Halloween or shopping. Community included volunteering, Life Skills camp, swimming lessons, and painting faces at a community event. These things either cost money, paid money, or were "yahoo" or "good job!" squares.

They then either "Applied for ODSP" or "Picked a Job". ODSP (Ontario Disability Support Program) pays $100 each time you pass the "pay day" squares, and Jobs paid more. I picked fun jobs like Camp Counsellor, High Sky Window Washer, Garbage Truck Driver, Dog Walker, Librarian, Cashier, Sandwich Artist, Rock Star, Babysitter, and Magician. They picked 3 out of a box and then picked their favourite. Kids are cute and they weren't necessarily picking the highest paying job!

They then just continued until the end, passing squares about community things and family things, like buying a gift for an uncle, going to the gym, learn to take bus, write a best selling book, win an award, buy a car, buy new shoes, see a hockey team play, help a puppy find its' home, forget parents birthday. These either paid, made you pay the bank, made you miss a turn, gave you a spin again, or were "good job!" squares. Mixed in there were about 6 "Pay days".

The last square was "Time to Relax and COUNT YOUR MONEY!". The money we used was Monopoly refill packs, but you could use camp bucks if you so desired!

STAFF RECOGNITION

PAPER ICE CREAM CONES
Each staff member had their name on a paper ice cream CONE shape on the wall. We added to each others' cone anytime by adding a scoop of ice cream (round ice cream scoop shaped paper).

Anyone could do this, it was quick to write a short note, and they were super cute when they started getting taller and taller!

SURPRISE SNACK
In my first communications with the staff, when finding out info for their 'bios', I also threw in the questions "What is your favourite camp appropriate beverage?" and "What is your favourite chocolate bar / candy?".

I picked up all of their favourites and served them at an evening meeting 2/3 the way through the summer. They were impressed that I "remembered" and called me "the best boss ever"!

THE CIVILIZED DINNER

One of our best activities on camp this year was a spur of the moment theme dinner. Some of the leaders decided that it would be good to have a quieter meal time, with less loud talking. So we came up with the "civilized" dinner.

It was really quite simple to set up. On the tables we place a vase with some flowers, and we found a CD with some classical music on it for background music. We had some conversation starter cards that we used for other activities that we placed in the middle of the table.

When the campers lined up for dinner, we explained how the meal would work. Campers would be only able to talk to people at their tables, and they had to talk in a conversational tone. We encouraged the leaders that were sitting on the tables to help with this.

It worked really well; the classical music in the background was a good effect as well. And it didn't take much to organize, we decided early afternoon and it was set up for dinner that night. The campers seemed to enjoy it as well, having a more settled meal.

CHRISTMAS IN JULY

I haven't done this event often, but it was a big hit last summer. I set it up in stations, and the kids could go and do whichever activity they wanted.

- Cookie decorating: we set out different colors of icing, sugar cookies, and lots of various kinds of sprinkles.
- Ornament making: paper, scissors, pipe cleaners, beads, strings, buttons, and any random things you can find. The kids get to make anything they can possibly think of.
- Snowflake making and Christmas cards: I put out construction paper, scissors, and markers. Then we showed the kids how to fold paper to make snowflakes. They could also make Christmas cards.
- Snowball fights: I had a huge box of fluff/stuffing, so I spread it out in a small corner for the kids to play in the 'snow'. It ended up spreading out to a large area, and could be slick if you weren't careful. But the kids really enjoyed making it snow, throwing it, and burying each other.
- Night Before Christmas: One of our staff set up a little story circle and read "T'was the Night Before Christmas".
- Carol singing: Some staff led caroling.
- Visit from Santa.

MISC-
- All of the activity staff dressed up as elves to run each station.
- We put some soft Christmas music on in the background.
- We played the fake fire place on the screen in the background.

MODERN ART NIGHT

We did this activity in stations.
- Finger painting
- Splatter painting: we taped up some butcher paper to the walls and let the kids have bowls of paint to throw.
- Michelangelo-style painting: I put paper on the bottom of some tables so that the kids could paint upside-down.
- Spin Art: we have a couple of the spin-art machines, so we set those out for the kids to drop paint in.
- Sculpting: I put out some clay and clay tools
- Self-Portraits: we set up a line of mirrors with mats out in front. The kids could sit and do self-portraits.
- Statue drawing: Some of the staff dressed up as statues and posed for the kids to draw.
- Origami: we found some simple instructions online.
- Marble painting: Using pie tins, the kids squirted paint on the paper and rolled marbles on top to make designs.

NOTE: This activity very quickly turned into messy night when some counselors decided to start throwing paint everywhere and at people. I would suggest establishing some expectations of staff before the activity. We often do plan messy nights, so expectations distinguishing the two activities might have been helpful.

BEACH THEME

OPENING SET-UP AND WELCOME
- Front of reception: A beach scene (palm trees / beach umbrella / fake beach scene / life guards, etc.)
- Inside set-up: A beach bar where announcements and sign-ups are made all week
- Counselors : Different types of beach stereotypes (muscle men in oil / beach bums / surfer dude / sun-tanners, etc.)
- Beach music playing at reception and the inside hall
- Inside games: indoor soccer / skating / friendship bracelets / 4square / trampolines

Some counselors need to be dressed in normal staff clothing helping with sign-ins, parental inquiries and inside activities (possible offering of surfer ankle bracelets to be handed out to campers)

GAMES and SPECIAL ACTIVITIES
- Word of the day : giving cabins surfer slang to use for the day and an all camp word for the day that the MC of the day will get camp to learn. These phrases and words will also be used in every activity, as well as at announcements at wake-up and breakfast.
- The "Aloha, bro!" posting board - This board will feature "the best of" photos and write-ups (best beach pose, best sunscreen face, best tan, best board shorts, best dive, etc.)
- Each cabin is to create a surfboard with cardboard or Styrofoam for cabin photos for the end of the week and final camp-fire (creation period TBA – possibly on late wake up Wednesday)
- Wake-up: wave forecasts done by the kids, Hawaiian style every morning.
- A smoothie making competition where all sorts of ingredients will be available for teams. Within the groups every kid has to make a smoothie, and amongst there peers will choose the best out of the group's to send as their submission to be judged. Garnish is worth extra points. Judges include a few staff and a few campers.

THEME DINNER: BEACH BONFIRE OR LUAU
- Chicken kebabs on a skewer (served on banana leaves)
- Hake and chips wrapped in banana leaves or in newspaper

Thereafter, a Glow-in-the-Dark (GITD) festival begins featuring the following activities:
- Limbo
- GITD Ultimate Frisbee
- GITD Volley ball
- Shell painting
- Glow toy releasing

Set-up: Portable music box (DJ equipment) / Paraffin / Juices / Drop-mats for chilled activities / wood-blitz / collected banana leaves
After the luau, kids gather by the bonfire for a on the beach traditional fire-show.

WE'RE ALL GOING M.A.D.

Welcome to M.A.D. week, the week focusing on Music, Arts, Drama and Dance!

OPENING SET-UP AND WELCOME
- For setup in front of reception we will have a mini stage covered in black and red
- We will also have a mini arts area where kids can come learn to do friendship bracelets
- As well as a chill area where there will be a capoeria circle
- Sign in's should look like a box office and each kid will get a ticket to enter camp. These tickets will be handed in to the infirmary on checking in and will be punched at each station. The kids will later use these tickets to gain entry to Camp Show on Saturday.
- Counselors will be acting out random skits and stunts on the stage in front and others will be dressed as mimes going around to the different cars and helping the kids.

GAMES and SPECIAL ACTIVITIES
- Flash-mob – The kids will be taught a flash-mob Dance by Magma which they will do every time the song comes on during the week.
- Theme in a Hat: In cabins kids will write down an object, or scene and then everyone will put theirs in a hat, they will go around the cabin drawing a piece of paper and will then have to become that thing and get the others to guess what it is.
- There will be fun improv games from Whose line is it anyway which the kids will volunteer for.
- Each counselor going to campout will have a basic knowledge and understanding of telling a story and will tell the kids how to do it. The kids will later prepare a short skit on a random topic that they'll draw out of a hat at the campsite and show it to the group. Around the campfire while having s'mores they will get a chance to tell a story of their own to the rest and hear some stories from the counselors as well.
- For the kids who decide to stay at camp instead there will be a hip hop workshop. The kids will learn all kinds of things relating to hip hop, such as Graffiti, Djing, Dance.
- They will also be given a brief workshop on how to become a believable character.
- So You Think You Can Dance? - Everyone will be split up into two crews, the first crew will work on their groups name and war cry while the other learns a simple dance routine, they will then change over. Once each Crew has rehearsed and made it their own, they will have a dance off. Seniors will battle seniors and juniors will battle juniors. And it'll be voluntary. If a kid does not want to battle they won't have to. But otherwise they can go up as many times as they'd like to show their moves. There will also be performances by the Dance class to make it really cool and individuals or group who have worked on a routine can also strut their stuff. For those who don't enjoy dance they can join a counselor as the Judges.
- At the end of the week there will be a camp show, a collaboration between Drama, Dance and Arts. The kids will be able to sign up for the drama classes every afternoon to participate with the drama aspect of the show. Magma's dance classes during the day will be incorporated into the show as well on the Friday class. Arts will be making some of the props and backdrops for the show.

THEME DINNER: ONE CRAZY NIGHT
- Tables will be arranged in a maze like pattern in the dining hall.

- Kids will be able to sit where they want and not in their cabins.
- Dinner served will be normal food eaten in completely unconventional ways. They will get a mini burgers and fries on a skewers stick. Ice cream and brownies with chopsticks.

OLD TIME OLYMPICS

The activities selected were badminton, marbles, jacks, and croquet. Jumprope was a big hit with the crowd. Everyone attempted to do double-dutch.

Each person could rotate on their own and select their activity. Staff was on hand to participate if a partner was needed. It was a fun time! Sno cones, popcorn and cotton candy were served.

TEACHABLE MOMENT

The counselor holds a carabiner and describes its uses and method it is used.

He or she explains its strength and that it will hold upwards of 5,000 pounds. But, in order for it to work it must open up so it can demonstrate its strength.

Everyone is in a circle and the carabiner is passed from person to person. Each person explains what they need to be more open about to help strengthen them.

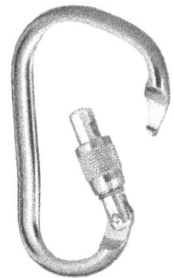

SURVIVOR THEME

MAKING THE TRIBES

Each team should have the same amount of players, with an equal number of campers from each age group. If the teams are uneven in numbers someone will have to sit out during each challenge. Once you have your teams explain to them that they are now a "tribe" and they have to come up with a tribal name and symbol.

COMPETITIONS

Lava Race
In this event a huge volcano has erupted in the tribes camp. The lava is slowly pouring in and the tribes must escape. This is a relay using potato sacks.

Kangaroo Relay
Island Kangaroos have challenged your tribe to a race. The tribe lines up in two lines, and the first two people have a gator skin ball. On the whistle the two put the ball in between their knees and hop down to the cone and back. All tribes go at once, two members at a time.

Jungle Walk
Tribes are lost in the jungle, they need to maneuver their way out of the jungle without losing anyone. Tribes pass five hula hoops down their class line of joined hands. If someone breaks hands they are lost in the jungle forever!!

Coconut Carry
Again tribes are in two straight lines. The first two carry the "coconut" (gator skin ball) between their foreheads, without using their hands, down to the cones and back, and then hand off to the next two members.

Escape
The tribes have been captured by another tribe and they have tied their legs together so they must figure out a way to escape. This is a five person three legged race. (five people are connected instead of two.)

Smoke Signal
You have decided that you need help to get off the island, send up your smoke signal (7 balls on a parachute) the quickest.

Water Balloon Toss
Toss the water-filled balloon back and forth to your partner. The other players will be doing this at the same time. If your water balloon breaks, you and your partner are out. Move the lines back as play progresses. The idea is for partners to have to throw the water balloon further and further to each other. The last pair with an unbroken water balloon wins.

Playground Obstacle Course
Tribe members will begin at the cargo net and once on the equipment go to the left and slide down the slide. Then while on the ground the tribe members will go to the monkey bars where

they must cross and reach the equipment then go to the right and slide down the slide on the left side (open and winding). Once on the ground again the tribe members will run to the rock wall and climb the wall then going to the left and sliding down the slide on the right.

Endurance Course
On a field set up a course that includes such things as stops to jump rope 10 times, do 5 cartwheels, and 10 jumping jacks. Each tribe member must go through the course.

Balancing Act
Tribe members are to place a Frisbee upside down in their head and get to the other end course and run back giving the Frisbee to another tribe member. Each tribe member must go through the relay.

Mental Challenge
Write a ten line Survivor poem about your tribe.

Food Challenge
Each tribe member must eat their snack provided with no silverware/plastic ware and take a tribe picture after completion.

Tribal Council Riddle
Now head to the place where you can find cold water and air conditioning.

TRIBAL COUNCIL
Tribal council was a great way to get the kids feelings and emotions to come out. We would talk to the children about their experience that week. Ask questions about sportsmanship, teamwork, who the children thought their team leader was and why. When awarding the idol that week be sure to involve the whole camp and stress good sportsmanship!

EMBERS: WISH-SURPRISE-WONDER

Age of campers: 13
Days into session: 3
Time allotted/actual: 45/90

Location:
Archery tree house

Props/Materials/Symbols:
- Candles
- Incense
- Tibetan singing bowl for starting ambiance as well
- Flash paper
- Flash cotton
- Charcoal
- Lighter fluid
- Lighter stick
- Popcorn and oil
- Popcorn popper that works over a fire (metal pole with special popcorn popper attachment)
- Flute / guitar
- Bowl for popcorn
- Refer to this reference
- http://campaugusta.org/Partnering/Development/Wish_Wonder_Surprise/wish_wonder_surprise.html

Prep done:
- Fire pit at tree house needs all the usual things for a fire to present in a location without ready water.
- Had all materials hauled out there earlier in the day
- Handy if someone can light the charcoal fire a few minutes before you arrive at the tree house (more surprising).

Opening/Mood set:
- Had designated camper light candles (one person's role per day)
- Everyone lit one piece of incense

Questions/Activities:
- On upper deck. Write down a wish on a piece of flash paper. The wish can't be personal or selfish – it must be for the greater good, be obtainable, and be something that you can influence. Wait until everyone is done. Play the flute for a minute. In silence, have everyone throw their paper into the candles – poof! Then, another wish is written down. Something that you want to let go of or release about yourself. If you have changed in some way at camp, or you want to change something about yourself. When it burns, it will be released.
- Go down to the fire pit and pull out the popcorn maker from under the deck. The oil

needs to completely coat the bottom of the pan. Move/shake the popcorn maker vigorously over the fire, or else the popcorn will burn. Likely need to make two batches. Pour the popcorn into a bowl.

- Go to the lower deck, lay down in a star pattern with heads in the center, but not touching. Hopefully, there are mattresses/cushions there to make it more comfortable. Play the wonder game. This game can for 5 minutes of 50 minutes, your call. About 20-30 minutes is fine.
  - Popcorn style (ha ha) a person says what they are wondering. The person simply starts by saying "I wonder . . ." and then whatever they wonder. Next person inspired to go begins by breaking the silence.
  - Wonders are not to be answered in any way/shape/form. Not verbally or nonverbally – asked of the universe.
  - Wonders are not to be followed up on, discussed later, or referred to by anyone in the cabin that night or later.
  - Also note to everyone that silence is allowed – 30 seconds of silence can be awkward, yet, be comfy with that until (and if) someone wants to speak, or speak again. The peace of looking at the stars in the woods and wondering in silence, or not wondering for a moment, is also magical.
  - It is generally helpful, but gauge your cabin, to not have the wonders be about someone else folks know.

Closing:
- Gather around the candles again.
- Ask what role wish, surprise, and wonder have in each of their lives. Can leave that as an open question, or, prompt.
  - How much of each? How much is created by the person, and how much is experienced?
  - Places experienced more or less?
  - Which one is enjoyed more or less?
  - How about at camp?
  - Can discuss what role they have in creativity and innovation.
  - What would be awesome about something each could change about their lives outside of camp to bring more of these into being?
- Play the Tibetan Singing Bowl for a minute as an ending, allowing the final ring to close the embers.

Breakdown:
- Put out the fire thoroughly
- Following day, have village leader collect everything.

Thoughts on pacing?
- It moved along with interest throughout, yet the campers wanted to take so much time with each segment, that it ended up taking a long time. Campers had a blast and listed it as one of their favorite embers.

ZOMBIE RAID - CAMP WIDE GAME

I ran a zombie themed overnighter that would make an epic all camp activity (assuming kids are of the right age, our program was for girls in 6th grade and up).

First, here's our blurb for our overnighter:
"In this Team Adventure Game (T.A.G.), the zombie pandemic has spread across to globe. Researchers are close to developing a cure to the virus, but will they succeed in time or fall victim to the virus themselves? You'll start this event by drawing to see who among you has contracted the virus; those left will join the last team of researchers. Your mission: avoid the zombies, find the other research stations, and salvage their research—you may be able to cure the disease! Keep your wits… and your brains, and you just might succeed in this overnight wide game. Don't forget a flashlight, this is an after dark game!" (T.A.G. games are what we call a series of tag-after-dark games that we offer for various age groups at various camps, including Spy Games, Super Hero Heist, and my baby, the Zombie Raid.)

Our game goals and rules were as follows:

Zombies Goal:
Tag humans to turn them into zombies! Zombies win by converting all of the human players.

Zombie Rules:
1. Zombies do not think! Have girls consider that if they question whether or not a zombie can do something. For instance, if a zombie finds a research station, she may be tempted to hide and wait nearby, since she knows humans will need to go inside. This demonstrates thought, "If I wait here, a human will come by." Since zombies don't think, they can't guard a research station.
2. Zombies don't run. Zombies are dead. They are clumsy. Their body acts in slow, jerky movements. Zombies may lurch forward in a couple sudden steps, but this should last for no more than three steps (right, left, right).
3. Zombies can not enter marked safe zones, but because of the scent of humans, they can guard safe zones hungrily.
4. All players must be in eyesight of a buddy at all times.

Human Goal:
Find three research stations and collect data CDs. Humans win by returning three CDs to the safe zone.

Human Rules:
1. Humans must wear a brightly colored headband across their forehead. If they get tagged, they must remove the headband. If any player loses her headband, she becomes a zombie, regardless of whether she has been tagged.
2. Each station has a tool that can help defend against the zombies. Directions on how to use the tool will be nearby. Players will need to be prepared to read and use context clues to figure out each tool.

3. Weapons affect humans, too! If caught using the weapon improperly, humans will have to do the action that the weapon inflicts. Zombies can call you out for misuse!
4. If you are tagged, return to the zombification station to apply make-up and return to play as a zombie.
5. All players must be in eyesight of a buddy at all times.

Set the scene right, for believability!
- Use a fingerprint scanning prank app to screen players wishing to enter the safe zone 9we don't want the virus infiltrating our defenses! We told girls that it was a biometric scanner.
- Hang warning signs, propaganda posters, and caution tape all over the place! Our safe zone was littered with propaganda posters found online. Use smoke machines and eerie light, if you've got access to such fanciness.
- Consider what roles you and the event volunteers will play. Options include: CDC Virus Control and Containment Team (we even made special id badges), lab scientists at each station (zombie or human), zombie hunters (patrolling with the kids and helping maintain safety), Security Agents (performing health screens at the entrance to the safe zone and/or maintaining safe zone perimeter), zombies (out with the kids to help maintain safety)

The humans found three weapons along the way. They were:
- Radiation Wands(foam insulation, painted bright green and glow in the dark) – zombie has to do ten dizzy bat spins if tagged with one
- Air-born Medication (flour bombs) – zombie closes eyes and counts to 50
- Healing Ointment (Vaseline with nasty smelling essential oils and neon food color mixed in) – can prevent a tagged human from turning into a zombie, if applied immediately. Can only be used once.

We weren't 20 minutes into the all night event before kids started asking when it would be offered again. It was by far, the most fun I've ever had at an event for this age group, and the evaluations showed the same thing from participants. I highly recommend taking advantage of the zombie craze for teen programming!

GAMES FOR A SUPERHEROES THEME

KRYPTONITE
Have the campers sit in a circle outside. A water balloon is passed back and forth across the circle from player to player. If a player fails to catch the balloon, or it breaks when they attempt to catch it, that player is out.

PASS the BOMB
Equipment:
- Bucket full of water balloons
- Sheets

Instructions:
Divide the campers into 2 teams and pair them up. Each pair gets a tea towel and each camper holds two corners of the towel. One side begins by placing a water balloon in the centre of their tea towel. The object is to toss the balloon from one pair to the other, with the opposing side catching the balloon on their towel. Kid's volley the water balloon back and forth till someone misses and the balloon breaks. This gives the other team a point.

THE CITIES ON FIRE
Equipment:
- 4 Buckets
- Sponges

Instructions:
Divide players into two teams. Place empty buckets for each team at other end of the field. Each team gets their own full bucket of water at the starting line. The object of the game is to transfer water from the starting line to the finish line bucket so that the fire can be put out. Each player gets a sponge to suck up water at the starting line and squeeze it out into the finish line bucket

AQUAMAN
Divide the players into 2 teams and line them up from start to finish line. Players each have a bucket in hand. A large bucket is available at the start line. The player closest to the water source scoops up a bucketful and pours it into the next players bucket. That player turns and does the same, and so on down the line. The last player dumps whatever water is left into the finish line bucket. The first team to fill their bucket is the winner.

IT COULD BE WORSE
Everyone sits around the fire and the leader starts by saying something like, "I almost slept in this morning." The next person says something like, "It could be worse, you could have been last." Then the next says something worse like, "It could've been worse than that, you could've been in your underwear.", and the next person tries to say something worse and so on along the circle

STUFFY GAME

Get all the campers who brought a toy to pile them up together. Blindfold the campers and get them to find their own toy

LIFT THE PAIL
Divide the group into smaller groups of five or six. Everyone removes their shoes and socks and sits on the ground in a circle around the bucket of water. They lift the bucket up with their feet and balance to see who can hold it up the longest.

SUPERMAN TAG
Mark two lines in the grass or play area, at least 20' apart. Pick one camper to be Superman, and have him or her stand in the middle of the play area between the two lines. The other players are the "bad guys," and they should stand behind one of the lines.

To start, Superman yells, "Up, up, and away!" All of the bad guys must try to run through the play area and across the other line without being tagged by Superman. If Superman tags a bad guy, that camper is caught and must hold hands with Superman during the next round.

As more players are caught, they join hands with Superman, extending his reach. Play continues until only one camper is left. That player gets to be Superman for the next round.

EXTERMINATOR
Set out the game area and spread several towels on the ground at various locations. These are the hospitals.

One child is the evil villain and is armed with a spray bottle of water. The other guests are the people and superheros. The villain tries to exterminate the people by spraying them with his bottle of venum potion. When a player is sprayed they must lay on the ground with their hands and feet in the air.

The superhero's rescue the injured person and bringing them back to life by carrying them by the arms and legs over to the hospital. The villain cannot blast the superheros while a rescue is taking place. Once placed on the blanket the person comes back to life and can rejoin the game.

SUPERMAN MUSCLE GAME
Equipment:
- Many Balloons (30–40)
- An Air Pump (optional)
- A Set of Adult-Sized Clothes for Each Team

Preparation:
- Blow up at least 30 small balloons

Instructions:
Divide the campers into teams of 3 or 4. Have each team choose one player to be "Superman." Place the balloons between the teams. Have each Superman put on a set of overalls over his/her clothes. Set a timer for 1 or 2 minutes.

When you say "Go," each team must stuff as many balloons as possible under their Superman's clothes. When the timer dings, remove the balloons from each Superman one at a time, counting to see who had the most muscles (popped balloons don't count). Award a prize to the winning team!

THE KIDS FROM MARS
- Set up two boundaries across from each other on a flat playing surface.
- Choose 2 campers to be "The Kids From Mars".
- They are 'it' and should begin the game in the middle of the 2 boundaries.
- The rest of the players should line up along one of the boundaries facing them.
- Play begins when "The Kids From Mars" chant, "We're the Kids from Mars and well steal your candy bars, if you're wearing…" and they will choose a colour or some item of clothing that a person is wearing.
- Any player wearing that colour must attempt to run across the playing field to get to the opposite boundary.
- If they are tagged before they reach the other side, they must sit in that spot and become a helper. They can tag players who run past them but they must remain seated.
- Those who make it across without being tagged can run again at the next chant.
- Play continues until everyone is tagged

SUPERHEROES
Campers spread themselves around the room and start moving around. The leader calls out the name of a superhero and the campers have to respond by acting as if they are that superhero.

Examples

Superman: Campers pretend to fly about in a superman pose, with one arm outstretched
Spiderman: Campers move around on fingertips and tiptoes, scurrying like a spider
Batman: Campers run with arms outstretched like bat wings
The Hulk: Campers stand and flex their muscles, while making an angry roar
Lara Croft: Campers run, jump and crouch on one knee
Scooby Doo: Campers huddle together in twos/threes saying "I'm scared shaggy"

IDEAS FOR A WILD WEST THEME

RULES OF CAMP
1. Follow the Wagon Trail – do not leave the Ranch
2. Clean yo Stables
3. Listen to the Sheriffs at all times
4. Do not talk to Bandits or Outlaws
5. Trot Slowly
6. Hog-tie your Hands to your side – no spitting, chewing or chuckin allowed
7. Golden Rule – Treat others as you would like them to Treat you

GAMES

BARNYARD TAG
Formation: Teams are lined up by the end line at a far end.
Depending on the number of children playing, split youth up into teams. Give the Players in the teams designated names: sheep, cows, horses, pigs...
- Two or three people are "It" in the middle of the room.
- "It" calls out the names of an animal (Example: Sheep)
- All sheep must run to the pen at the opposite end of the room without being caught.
- When barnyard is called, everyone must run to opposite ends.
- Penalty for being caught is to run all around the barnyard (A LAP OF THE GYM ONCE) and then they can come back in the game!
- Every few minutes - change the "Its".

DRESS A SCARECROW AND RUN
- Stock up on over-sized plaid shirts, goofy pants, rope belt, floppy hats and any other clothing that a scarecrow might wear.
- Make piles containing one of each item.
- The number of piles is determined either by the number of kids or teams participating.
- Line up kids and let the game begin!
- The children run to the pile, put on the outfit, and dart back to the starting line.
- If doing it as a team game, they would then switch the outfit with their teammate-who run out and back.
- First team with their last team member DRESSED AS A SCARECROW wins.

DUCKS AND COWS
To go along with your 'farm theme'....this is a great way to divide children into two teams.
- Players close their eyes while one person taps them on their shoulders and designates them either a "duck" or "cow."
- On a given signal, keeping their eyes closed the players must make their animal sounds to gather into their two teams.
- The ducks "quack" and the cows "moo."
- Begin the game when the two groups all "find each other.

DUCK WALK RACE
- Have children line up at the Start Line, squat down and grasp their ankles with each

hand from behind.
- On GO, they waddle to a designated Finish Line.
- They can't let go of their ankles or they're disqualified.
- The first child over the Finish Line is the winner... (This would be fun to play with "waddle music"

FARMER MAY I? (Played like Mother May I?)
- All the children line up side by side except the player who is the caller.
- The caller stands at a distance from the lined up players.
- He/she calls on each player in turn to take a number of steps toward him. The steps allowed are: baby steps, giant steps, and scissor steps (like forward jumping jacks.)
- The player answers "Farmer, may I?"
- The Farmer answers "Yes, you may." The player takes the prescribed number of steps toward the caller. If the player forgets to ask permission after they get directions--- and takes steps toward the caller--- they are sent back to the starting line.
- The first player to reach the caller is the winner and new caller.

SHEEP HERDING
- Before the event, inflate two white balloons.
- Attach short pieces of black curling ribbon to make sheep tails and use a black marker to draw faces on them.
- To play, divide players into two teams.
- Give the first player on each team a broom, or fly swatter, that they will use to herd their team's sheep across the room and back to the next player in line.
- The first team to finish herding their sheep wins! (You may want to have "sheep" clones ready in case the originals pop.)

MILK A COW
- Draw a cow on the wall and attached a rubber glove filled with milk.
- Poke holes in the finger so the milk will come out--the fingers are udders.

Another version of a MILKING GLOVE:
- Fill white surgical gloves with water and tie the tops.
- Put pinpricks in the ends of the fingers and attach to the clothesline.
- Children can now try and 'milk' their cow.

SIFTING FOR GOLD
- Have children pretend to be gold miners.
- Paint very small rocks, gold.
- Hide them in the sand.
- Give your children small sifters to sift through the sand looking for gold.

- If desired, have the kids trade the nuggets in for prizes

SACK RACE

If you are lucky enough to have a feed supply store near by, burlap sacks can be purchased inexpensively. If not, old pillow cases will do. A soft grassy park or lawn will prevent scrapes. (I purchased sacks at Oriental Trading.)

- Each player steps into his/her sack with both feet.
- Pull the sack high enough to hold the edges.
- Practice hopping first, until all of the players get the hang of it.
- Identify the start and finish lines.
- Blow the whistle and go!
- Adjust the race with obstacles for more excitement, or if it's summer, add sprinklers.

PLAY HORSESHOES

In case you haven't played in awhile, Horseshoes is an outdoor game played between two people (or two teams of two people) using four horseshoes and two throwing targets (stakes) set in a sand area. Each side takes turns tossing their 'shoes' to the other side at the stakes in the ground.
The closest one to the target wins.

The aim is to get a 'Ringer' which means to wrap the Horseshoe around the post when it is thrown. (It is traditional to place stakes 30-40 feet apart; however, when playing with younger children, place the posts closer to each other.) The game pieces are traditionally metal--however rubber sets are sold for younger children.

Scoring:
- 1 point is given for each horseshoe that is closer to the stake than the opponent's horseshoe.
- 3 points are given for each "ringer". (Pair 1 both throw their horseshoes and then pair two throw theirs.)
- Continue playing until one team reaches the 21-point goal. (Or what the children decide the goal will be)

PASS THE CORN GAME

Divide the children into two teams (or as many as you need) and have them form two lines. You will need a cob of dried Indian corn for each team.

- At the signal "go", the corncob is to be passed from child to child. The catch is that they can use any part of their bodies, except their hands.
- If the corn touches the ground at any time, it must go back to the beginning of the line again.
- Whichever team manages to get the corn to the end of the line first wins the game.
- The corn can also be used in a relay, with the kids putting the corn between their knees, and racing "crab" style.

"TRADITIONAL GAMES" with a Western Twist!

- Instead of 'Simon Says' play "THE RANCHERS SAYS"...or "THE COWBOY/COW-GIRL SAYS"...
- Instead of Old McDonald Had a Farm...Sing "OLD MCDONALD HAD A RANCH", complete with very loud sound effects. Each child or section can be given a different animal to act out.
- Instead of Mother May I? play "COWBOW OR RANCHER MAY I?"
  - All the children line up side by side except the player who is the caller.
  - The caller stands at a distance from the lined up players.
  - He/she calls on each player in turn to take a number of steps toward him. The steps allowed are: baby steps, giant steps, and scissor steps (like forward jumping jacks.)
  - The player answers "Cowboy, may I?"
  - The Cowboy answers "Yes, you may." The player takes the prescribed number of steps toward the caller. If the player forgets to ask permission after they get directions--- and takes steps toward the caller--- they are sent back to the starting line.
  - The first player to reach the caller is the winner and new caller.

- Instead of "Duck, Duck, Goose" play "COW, COW, HORSE"
- Instead of "Drop the Clothespin in the Bottle"--play DROP THE SNAKE IN THE BOOT or COWBOY HAT!

Materials:
- Cowboy Boot or hat
- flexible rubber or plastic snakes

Directions:
- Place a cowboy boot or cowboy hat on the ground.
- If children are young, have them stand over the boot/hat and drop the snake in the boot. In the original clothes pin version of the game--the child would kneel on a chair. He/she would face the back of the chair. A large-mouthed bottle would be directly below the back of the chair--where the children would drop the clothespin straight down. The child with the most clothes pins in the bottle won.
- Have older children stand farther back and attempt to toss it into the boot or hat.

BARNYARD or RANCH YARD
(This could also be called Zoo, Ocean, Circus, or Outer Space, if you are having a "Theme". You'd just change the names to go with the theme and adjust the team names.)
- Depending how many children you have--form teams. You can have anywhere from 3 Teams to ?????
- Teams are in their groups and one end of the gym.
- Players in teams have designated names: Sheep, Cows, Horses, Pigs, etc. (Any animal that is on a ranch)
- Two or three persons are "It" in the middle of the room.
- "It" calls out the names of the animals (Example - Sheep)
- All sheep must run to the pen at the opposite end of the room without being caught.
- When "BARNYARD" is called, everyone must run to the opposite end.
- Penalty for being caught is to run all around the barnyard (a lap of the gym) once--- and then they can come back in the game! (Remember to change the "It" people)

ART and CRAFT IDEAS

HAND PRINT HORSES
Need: Brown paint, paper, brown marker
1. Take brown paint and paint a child's hand.
2. Press the hand down on paper--WITH fingers pointing down.
3. The fingers are the legs and the thumb is the head.
4. Draw the mane and hoofs; add eyes and tail.

The image here is the Self-Adhesive Ranch Handprint Keepsake Craft Kit from Oriental Trading.

FARM WEAVING
Materials:
- Chicken Wire
- tape
- natural raffia
- gingham ribbon
- old blue jeans
- etc.

Directions:
1. Cut squares of small-holed chicken wire.
2. Put masking tape around the sharp edges.
3. Set out assorted lengths of natural raffia, gingham ribbons and narrow strips ripped from old blue jeans.
4. The children weave them in and out of the holes.

ANIMAL CRACKER PIN (Horses, sheep, cows, etc.)
Materials:
- animal crackers
- flat backed pins
- clear nail polish or varnish
- craft glue
- paint (optional)

Directions:
1. To begin coat your animal cracker with the polish or varnish in a well ventilated area and let it dry.
2. Next glue it to a pin.
3. If using paint have campers paint first, let dry and then cover with coats of clear nail polish.

I'M A COWBOY/COWGIRL!
Draw around child's body on a very large sheet of paper.
From this point you can go three ways.
1. Have the children draw on western gear, Cowboy hat, shirt vest, bandanna, jeans, boot, etc. They'll look cute taped around the room..
2. You could also use the traced body shape and dress it much like a collage.
   - Draw and color on a shirt. Next--Use brown paper/grocery bags to make and glue on a vest and chaps.

- Add a bandana made from napkins or paper with a western pattern. Can they make 'cowboy' hat shapes?
- Finish off with boots made from brown or black construction paper.

3. MAKE A COLLAGE: Using the blank body shape, fill it in with anything and everything to do with the theme.
   - Put magazines and more magazines on your parent's wish list. (Make sure the request goes out only for 'appropriate magazines)
   - Have children look for and cut out pictures of cowboys, anything from western or frontier days, horses, cows, sheep, open land, mountains, rivers, sunsets, camp fires, marshmallows, franks and/or beans, farm houses, ranches, line dancing, boots, jeans, cowboy hats, barns, rodeos, bandanas, huitar, fiddles (violins), upright piano, cabins, anything Indian, etc.

LASSO ROPE COLLAGE

Material:
- thin rope
- card stock or heavy paper
- glue

Directions:
1. Dip short lengths of clothing line into a bowl of glue.
2. On card stock, loop and place the rope onto the paper, trying to shape it into a lasso.
3. Allow to dry completely.

KIDS SWAP MEET

Send home a small flyer with the kids a few days before your Swap Meet outlining the rules etc. My flyer has included: Bring in 1 shopping bag of toys or books that you would like to swap. Parents have to approve what is in the bag. Only bring items that you want to swap, because, once an item is swapped it is swapped!

On the day of the event, kids bring in their bags of goodies and set them aside, not accessing them until the event takes place. For the event we mark out little areas on the floor or cement, approx. 3'x3', assign a space to each child, and they spread out their goods. Before swapping begins we remind kids, that once an item is swapped, it is swapped, so be sure they want an item or want to get rid of the item. Kids don't have to make a swap if they don't want to.

The counselors do a little skit on how to swap and then...Let the swapping begin.

Kids will usually sit next to a friend and then they take turns going around and swapping or you can have half the group get up and swap and then switch. It usually regulates itself pretty well.

We also play music and have popcorn. We have had no bad experiences with this and the kids have a great time. At the end of the day everything must go home.

THE PROPOSAL

Our last day of day camp is one of our busiest days. It is also a bittersweet day. I'm glad For the summer to be over but I'm also sad that it is. We do a variety of things to make this day spectacular (or at the very least fun).

SCHEDULE OF THE DAY (will be broken down later)
- 7-9 Choice Time
- 9:00 am Meet at Flag
- 9:15-12:30 Boy/Girl Day
- 12:30-1:15 Lunch
- 1:15-3:00 Group Time
- 3:00-3:15 Wedding
- 3:15-4:00 Dance
- 4:00 pm Meet at Flag
- 4:00-4:30 Snack
- 6:00 pm Camp Closes

Meet at Flag
- At 9:00 all three groups stand in a circle at the flag pole to say the Pledge.
- "The Proposal" takes place

"THE PROPOSAL"
This is a brief back and forth between a male and female counselor. Only the staff knows what is really going on. The climax is when the male staff gets down on one knee and asks the female to marry him.

Head Counselor: Today is our last day of camp. Does anyone have anything to say about that?

Random Counselor: I'm so sad today is the last day. I'm gonna miss you all. [Fake Cries]

Male Counselor: I have something to say.

Head Counselor: OK _____ (insert name) what is it?

Male Counselor: Well over the past _____ weeks I've got to know a lot of the kids and staff pretty well. I know that _____ can do _____ and the _____ is afraid of _____. But one person in particular has really caught my eye. This staff member has made me fall head-over-heels in love with her. She is really special and I want to spend the rest of my life with her.

[Walks over to the female counselor and gets down on one knee]

Male Counselor: _____ will you marry me?

[Crowd Gasps]

Female Counselor: Yes _____ I will marry you. [Applause from the crowd]

Head Counselor: Well kids it looks like we've got a wedding on our hands. What I need now is for the boys to go with _____ and the girls to go with _____.

The proposal ends with the group being split into boy and girl groups. Now the gender day begins.

BOY/GIRL DAY
This part of the day allows the boys to be bachelors and do "manly things" while the girls are bachelorettes and do "girly things." This lasts until lunch time (12:30).

Boys:
- Practice shaving on balloons
- Shaving cream relays
- Making sandwiches
- Burping contest
- Arm wrestling contest
- Checking out cars
- Playing football

Girls:
- Painting nails
- Fixing up hair
- Making the bride's dress (from toilet paper of course!)
- Making salad
- Dance contest/Gymnastics
- Hula-Hooping contest

LUNCH
Lunch can be done a variety of ways. What we do is order a big sandwich from Walmart and cut into lots of pieces. To go along with the sandwich we have chips and lemonade. We invite the parents of the campers along too, so we end up with a picnic at the front of the school. The headstart program at the school is also in session so they are invited as well. Overall we have about 200 people attend. After the lunch we show a slideshow of the summer for about 10 minutes. Make sure you have great music to go along with the slideshow; otherwise the younger campers will be bored.

GROUP TIME
During the summer we have three groups based on grade; Willows (K-2), Maples (3-5), and Oaks (6-8). It's important that even on the last day they get to spend time with their group. We allowed about an hour and a half for the groups to be together "one last time." The choices are really endless how you spend that time. What I like to do is have a "quote paper" that I've kept the whole summer and read the hilarious sound bites from camp, etc. to my group. I also play the "who am I?" game to see how well the campers know each other. Finally I spend time reminiscing with them. We talk about favorite trips, games, songs, etc. that we did during the weeks before. Make sure that you take a group picture to have for your memory books.

THE WEDDING
The whole purpose of the day is the wedding. We set it up like a real wedding. All the groups

meet at the flag and sit in sections. The head counselor is the Justice of the Peace and will marry the couple. The groom and his best man walk up to the "altar" and wait for the bride to appear. Next the music plays "Here Comes the Bride" as the bride and maid-of-honor walks with her to the "altar." After that the ceremony begins.

Head Counselor: Today we are here to watch the beautiful union between _____ and _____.
Head Counselor: _____ would you like to say anything about _____?

Groom: Yes, I would. [Improvises about their summer together]

Head Counselor: That's wonderful. _____ would you like to say anything about _____?

Bride: Yes. [Again improvising about their summer]

Head Counselor: That's very touching _____. Great stories and memories from both of you.

[Crowd AWWWWWS]

Head Counselor: OK, do you _____ take _____ to be your woefully wedded wife?

Groom: I do.

Head Counselor: And do you _____ take _____ to be your woefully wedded husband?

Bride: I do.

Head Counselor: [Hands them each a cup/bucket of water] Then I now pronounce you camp husband and wife. You may now douse your spouse. [Pours water on each other]

[The youngest campers throw grass onto the couple]

[Crowd Applauses]

Head Counselor: Alright kids let's get this party started!!!

CAMP DANCE
Since the summer is almost done we have most of our rooms packed up. One of the rooms has been set up at the "reception hall." Here is where the dance will take place. It's not a formal dance and it's supposed to be silly and fun. This also gives the bride and groom a chance to change into clean clothes. Make sure you've got great music and take lots of pictures of the event.

FLAG/END OF DAY
After the dance is over everyone meets one last time at the flag pole. We take down the flag and each group gives a paper-plate award for each kid. Finally they tell who their camper of the summer was. After that we have snack (for today its cookies and punch) and have choice time until 6. Then at six o'clock I lock the doors and camp is closed.

CLOSING THOUGHTS
Wow this day is packed!!! There are a couple skits, a wedding, a dance, a gender day, and time for reminiscing too. The key for this day being successful is (like many things) staff willing to

play along. They are going to feel silly but that is okay, its summer camp! We went over this day at our weekly planning meeting on Wednesdays. Since we plan a week in advance, this week was already planned out so all we talked about was how this day was going to work. There are logistical things that need to be thought about like room usage and what to do if it rains. The truth is that not every camp may be able to run this activity exactly as it's laid out here. Then again I WANT you to add your OWN ideas to this day. Make it your own. This is merely a template. I hope that you enjoy this day and that the kids do as well. It is one of my favorite days of the summer, albeit the saddest one too.

ACKNOWLEDGMENT

A huge special thanks to all the round table contributors whose submissions were chosen to be in this book.

Gary Forster
Cody Thatcher
Elaine Shepherd
Linda Dillon
Robyn Holmlund
Kim Darcy
Nikki Stone
Messody Ezagui
Sally Schaaf
Elana M.
Cory Harrison
Diane Wheeler
Beverly Anne Baldrey
Dawn Rudolph
David Mitnick
Kelly Sifford
Theresa Rogoff
Kimberly Mallory
Joshua Reynolds
Denise Secor
Paula DeTellis
Trevor Kavanagh
Deb Simpson
Johanna Sievers
Mary Siniard
Philip Drake
Megan Catlin
Kristen Widenmaier
Joe Carter
Samantha Lucheck
Jason Eng
Mark "Bambam" Leonor
Stephanie "Captain" Williams
Rebecca Simpson
Courtney Smith
Jeremy Maahs
Erin Hollen
Mark "Old Man" Pearlman
Robyn Bruton
Shanelle Lambert-Rauh
Joan Wells
Janet Russell

Victoria Ketteringham
Tory Thelen
Tara Jones
Colleen McGourley
Siobhan Morland
Sandi Smoot
Shelley Mitchell
Rosemarie Lynch
Maureen Dowell
Lori Gjovig
Lori Schoenhard
Linda Martin
Leah Ferrassoli
Laura Janis
Katie Lange
Kelly Wilson
Kaylahree Mayfield
Katie Sutliff
Josh Maag
Kim Koopman
Jeannine Ryan
Janet Keller
James Himstedt
Heidi Wodrich
Graeme McCafferty
Wayne Stewart
Diana Fong
David Brizius
Christie Comeau
Craig Rubinstein
Caterina Maw
Carrie Cullum
Bri
Brendon Pirie
Alex Sego
Lee "Sprout" Sheehan
Sophie Duncan
Randall Grayson, Ph.D.
Sarah Erickson
Catherine Collins
Patty Levan